Young Revolutionary – A Teen's Guide to Activism

Published by: Chanice Lee, in partnership with YBF Publishing, LLC.

www.chanicelee.com

Manufactured in the United States of America

Cover Photo by: Carrie Feit, Carrie Feit Portraits

Cover Design by: Arriale Henry, A. Henry Media.

Edited By: Nia Sadé Akinyemi, The Literary Revolutionary.
www.theliteraryrevolutionary.com

ISBN #: 978-0-9968910-6-6

Follow Author Chanice Lee

Facebook/Instagram/Twitter: @ChaniceALee

www.chanicelee.com

Young Revolutionary:
A Teen's Guide to Activism

By: Chanice Lee

YBF
PUBLISHING

ATLANTA   MIAMI   NEW YORK   DMV   DALLAS   OKC

Dedication

For every teenager who aspires to make change in this world.

Table of Contents

WHAT IS
ACTIVISM?

Activism is the policy or action of using vigorous campaigning about political or social change.

Notice how nowhere in the above definition does it state that activism requires you to be a certain age, because it doesn't. There is no minimum age to be an activist. Whether you believe it or not, being clear about that fact is one of the most important things you will take away from this book. If you walk around with a mindset that says, *"I'm too young to pay attention to that"* when referring to various world issues, you will have a hard time trying to make change in the world. This book will teach you the ins and outs of activism and most importantly how I can help guide you to becoming the best teen activist possible!

The teenage years are an interesting time in life. Most people are under the impression that the only responsibility of a teenager is to simply live life without a care in the world, and enjoy being young. Please do not fall into this trap. How will change ever be made if no-one cares about anything? Sometimes, I look around and think to myself, "Why aren't there more people my age who care about the same things I do? Who care about what's going on in the world? Who actually want to make change?" Then I thought, "Maybe there are teenagers who truly do want to make change, but they just don't know where to get started." That's where the idea for *Young Revolutionary* was born.

Young people are the future. It is up to us to be and create the changes in order to see a brighter future for ourselves and for future generations to come. As fast as times are changing, we are the ones who should be at the forefront of social and political movements. We have no choice but to be the change-makers, the innovators, and the leaders.

Imagine how different the world would be if every teenager knew they had the power to make change? The purpose of me writing this book is to create a clear cut guide for teenagers interested in changing the world. This book is not intended for teenagers who are interested in being "normal", "average", or *mediocre*. This book is for teens who aren't afraid to stand out and teens who are willing to take risks to do what it takes to create change. If you're one of those teens currently reading this, then congratulations you are on the right path! The goal of this book is for every young person to recognize and unleash their greatness.

Now, I'd like to explain that this book is NOT a "how-to" manual. This is a *guide* that I created based upon my personal experiences on my journey as a youth activist, combined with extensive research that I figured would be a huge help to other teens like me. This book is filled with information. How you interpret it and how you choose to use the information is completely up to you. Activism comes in many shapes and forms, so feel free to carve your own path on the journey to unleashing your greatness.

STEP 1

IDENTIFY YOUR
PASSION

What do you absolutely love doing? What can you talk about or think about for hours without getting tired of it? What do you feel is a part of your destiny? Your purpose? Whatever comes to your mind when you think of these things may just be your passion. Your passion is not always something that you love. It could be something that makes you so angry to the point where you feel you absolutely have to do something about it. In some cases, discovering your passion can happen as a result of a tragedy.

I vividly remember it being the summer before my 8th grade year that I learned my passion. Seeing the uproar on social media happen over the death of Sandra Bland was the start. Sandra Bland was a 28-year-old Black Woman who was found hanging in a jail cell in Waller County, Texas, on July 13, 2015, just three days after being arrested during a traffic stop. I watched the video of her arrest and I felt a stinging in my chest. All I could think was, *"Why is this Police Officer handling her so brutally as if she's an animal? Why is he yelling and screaming at her for no reason?"*

I was thirteen at the time and I didn't know what to do, but I felt like I had to do *something*. So, just like the millions of other outraged Twitter users, I tweeted #JusticeForSandraBland as an act of solidarity, then signed a petition that demanded that the Department of Justice investigate her death. That's when everything changed for me.

During that same summer, another incident occurred. There was a video floating around the internet of a large group of Black teenagers at a pool party in McKinney, Texas. They were racially profiled by white police officers. All I saw in the video were the teenagers scrambling, screaming, and in a complete state of fear as several police officers pulled out their guns on them. One child in particular, a 15-year-old Black girl, was thrown onto the ground with excessive force by a police officer, as she screamed that he was hurting her back. Witnessing the video of that incident really hit home for me because I automatically thought to myself, "*What if that were me?*" The mere possibility of such horrible things ever being done to me was enough for me to decide what I truly cared about.

For me, constantly being exposed to racism and police brutality sparked my passion for activism. They aren't the greatest things to talk about, but there came a point where I realized I didn't have a choice but to. These things directly affected me, so I felt it would be foolish of me to pretend as if it didn't and ignore them. I started learning as much as I could to become more socially aware on issues I felt I needed to be paying attention to. I didn't quite fully understand the concept of activism or what being an activist truly meant yet. At the time, all I knew was that I was a 13-year-old girl who was sick and tired of constantly witnessing injustices.

When I was 14, I decided to fully immerse myself into activism. I felt that I was at a place where I had enough confidence to actually do something about the things I'd started to care about. I made it my business to learn, learn, and learn some more. I eventually thought to myself, *I've seriously got to do something now.* I felt as if it were my duty to make some type of change in this world and to this day I still feel the same way. I wasn't quite sure then how I would do it, I just knew it was something I had to achieve. Ever since then my life has completely changed.

If you're not quite sure what your passion is, no worries! One thing I can suggest is to experiment. Try new things, be open to doing something you've never done before, and you just might discover your newfound passion. If you're having trouble experimenting with new things, ask yourself, "How can I serve?" Think of an issue that is affecting you, your community, or the world that drives you to want to do more. That's one place you can start. Start thinking, *what can I do to come up with a solution for this problem?* and let your mind do the brainstorming from there.

As you identify your passion, it is necessary that you let your intuition guide you. By that, I simply mean trust yourself. In my experience, simply choosing to follow my passion has taken me places and brought me opportunities I would have never imagined. Realize that whatever your passion may be is no mistake. Whether it be advocating for Women's Rights, Racial Justice, or bettering the environment through Environmentalism, you were led to that path because it was meant for you. *You* define your passion. *You* define your greatness. *You* define your purpose. The most important thing is that you realize *why* you're fighting for what you're fighting for and that you stand firm on your morals, beliefs, and goals. Changing the world is not easy, but I am a strong believer in passion fueling success and that doing what you truly love always produces the best results.

STEP 2

EDUCATE YOURSELF ON THE CAUSE

Activism can be a bit overwhelming at first, and you may find yourself asking, "Where do I even start?" Well, with activism comes learning and I promise you there will be a whole lot of it. Don't expect yourself to automatically be an expert. Understand that you will constantly be taking in new information on this journey as an activist.

Before you start to educate yourself, you have to operate in the mindset of *wanting* to learn. The information will not simply come to you. You will be doing a lot of looking and searching. The good part is that there are many ways and resources for you to do so!

Read

As a Teen Activist, you need to be armed with facts, so now is the time to stock up on books. If you're not much of a book person, there are many other options for reading, such as online blogs, magazines, and digital newspapers. Read as much as you can! Read to stay updated on what's going on in the world. Read what will help you deepen your understanding on activism. Read cause-related books that provide an in-depth analysis of a particular movement or cause and the issues it grapples with. Read, Read, Read!

Research

Researching can come in many forms, but the most popular type in this day and age is using the internet. Since technology is so easily accessed, you can find out anything you want at the tap of a search button. When using the internet for research I recommend using Google Scholar. Google Scholar is described as the *scholarly web to discover articles, books, and more from academic publishers and research institutions.*

Here are some other methods of gathering information when researching:

- Interviews
- Questionnaires/Surveys
- Study existing documents, forms and reports
- Focus groups (Group discussions)

Find Reliable News Sources

Make sure that when keeping up with certain news sources they are not satirical, biased, or one-sided. In this day and age, national news is easily accessible through social media. The news is literally available at the click of a follow button!

Listen to Others Who Are Knowledgeable

Chances are whatever you're interested in, there is someone who is an expert and has an extensive background of research and knowledge on the subject. You would be surprised how much you can learn just by listening to those who know what they're talking about!

Attend Educational Workshops, Conferences, Seminars, and Summits

I would strongly suggest searching for upcoming educational workshops, conferences, seminars, or summits near you that you can attend. Local social and political organizations usually host workshops for the general public that you can be a part of. There are even some conferences, seminars, and summits solely for young people that you can be a part of if you seek them out.

Take a Class

Let's say, for example, you're interested in Women's Studies, Politics, or a specific subject that is likely to be taught as a course. You can reach out to the Professor at your nearby college and ask if you can sit in on the class for a day.

We are currently in the age of information, therefore, there is no excuse for ignorance. If you have access to an electronic device, or to the internet in general, try your best to use it to your advantage rather than spending all of your time on frivolous activity, such as entertainment. It will be worth it!

STEP 3

PUT YOUR PASSION INTO ACTION

When people think of the word "activist" they tend to think of a militant protester marching down the street holding up signs, while yelling out of a bullhorn. This image often tends to intimidate teenagers, but it shouldn't! Although that is what activism is for some people, it is not an accurate representation of activism as a whole. There are many everyday things that you can do to make a difference whether they are small or complex.

Once you have identified what your passion is and you have begun learning more about it, the work begins. Activism requires you to *act*, and doing so can happen in a variety of ways. It is your responsibility to figure out the most effective way for you to demonstrate that you truly do care about your cause. You can talk about how passionate you are about a certain subject, but the best way to create change is to actually do something about it!

Advocacy is any action that speaks in favor of, recommends, argues for a cause, supports or defends, or pleads on behalf of others. If you're new to activism, it can be a bit tricky figuring out the best way to advocate for your cause. I feel the following information would be helpful for a teen activist like you.

Establish a Goal and Create a Vision

Activism comes with a purpose, which means that anything you do related to activism should not be done aimlessly. This is why you want to establish a goal so you can create a mind map of how you plan on achieving your goal and what you're going to do to get there. Think to yourself, as an activist, *what do I envision as the end goal or result of my efforts, hard-work, and advocacy?* Asking yourself this question should help you come to a clear conclusion. Shifting to a goal-oriented mindset can help you create a precise vision of what you want to achieve.

Personally, when it comes to activism, everything I do is with the intent to educate, inspire, and empower. If I feel that something doesn't fit into those three categories, then there isn't any point of me doing it. Always remember to do everything with a purpose. If you can't think of a purpose, then chances are you probably shouldn't be doing it. When you start making others aware of the injustice you've identified, what action are you hoping to encourage? It could be that you want to gain signatures for your petition in support of a proposed plan for the administration, or perhaps you're more interested in raising public awareness. Either way, listing short, intermediate and long-term goals keeps you organized and shows supporters you've thought things out. Always be intentional about the things you do.

Use Your Voice

It is common for a teenager to feel like their voice is not being heard, but in reality your voice is a lot more powerful than you think. If you care about something, then let the world know! Don't ever be afraid to speak out for what you believe in. As long as it is not harming anyone in any way, speak up and out!

TEEN ACTIVIST SPOTLIGHT

Kristen Woods, 15, says:

"It is important for teens to speak their minds, because we represent the next generation of voters and leaders in this nation. We are paying full attention to what is happening around us and by speaking out, we prove that we are willing to be involved and work for positive and meaningful change."

Alter Your Everyday Behavior

It's not just about what you say, it's about what you do. For example, if you're an environmental activist you would want to implement practices that don't harm the environment like using paper instead of plastic. If you're against oppression of all forms, then look out for marginalized groups and be the best ally that you can. You have to practice what you preach and lead by example. Words may be powerful, but your behavior and actions speak volumes.

TEEN ACTIVIST SPOTLIGHT

Brooklyn Converse, 16, says:

"Making activism a part of my life has helped me realize who my true friends are. I noticed how cruel a lot of them were and I didn't want their negativity a part of my life. It has also made me want to inspire my true friends and educate them to become activists as well. The same goes for my family. Activism made me want to change their perspective of the world."

Utilize your personal skills.

What are you good at? What do people come to you for because they know they can count on you for it? Think about it. Whatever comes to your mind can somehow be incorporated into your activism and advocacy work. Trust me!

REAL LIFE EXAMPLE:

THE MELANIN DIARY
SOCIAL JUSTICE. HISTORY. POLITICS. EMPOWERMENT.

I'm a writer, so I decided to start my blog *The Melanin Diary* back in March of 2017. My motto is, *"Social Justice, History, and Politics, from the Black Teen's perspective"*. I write articles pertaining to those topics, while also engaging in online activism. I make it a point to achieve my three goals: "to educate, inspire, and empower." I sat down and thought to myself, *how can I effectively utilize my personal skills to make change in this world while also achieving my personal goals?* Now, here I am writing my first book. See how it all goes hand in hand?

If you think hard enough of how to incorporate your personal skills into activism, you'll realize that you really can do what you love or what you're good at, while also making change!

Attend a Protest, March, or Demonstration.

Don't like something? Then do something about it and make it known (peacefully of course)! Protests, Marches, and Demonstrations are a great way to be within a large group of people who all care about the same things you do. It's also a great way to have your voice heard. Usually when there is a major occurrence that generally upsets people, protests, marches, and demonstrations will start to appear. If you feel that is something you want to be a part of, then go for it! When attending a protest, march, or demonstration, always go with someone you trust. Protests can get pretty rowdy or violent sometimes, so it's important that you remain as peaceful and calm as possible.

REAL LIFE EXAMPLE:

My first major march was the Florida March for Black Women. I didn't really know what to expect, but it turned out to be amazing! I also ended up being the youngest speaker, which was such a liberating moment for me. I spoke in front of about one thousand people and I had the chance to speak from my heart to say what I felt needed to be heard and what was important to me.

Learn How to Lobby

Lobbying is seeking to influence a politician or public official on an issue. Is there a law that you want changed, a bill that you desperately want to become a law, or an issue in your community that you don't like? Your elected officials are the people you need to know. From my experience, members of Congress are especially interested in Teen lobbyists. They seek input from fresh, young voices that care about issues affecting the world.

- You can find your **Representative** by going to house.gov and typing in your zip code.
- You can find your **Senators** by going to senate.gov and selecting your state.

<u>The 3 Most Popular Ways to Lobby Include:</u>

Calling Your Member of Congress

Whether it be your Representative or Senator, you can either call the Washington, D.C. office or you can call your local office of your Member of Congress. When calling, it is important to know that your Senator or Representative will not be answering the phone themselves, but one of their staff members will. When the actual conversation is happening just remain calm and concise. Introduce yourself, state what you're in support for or opposed of, and explain why that issue is important to you.

REAL LIFE EXAMPLE:

For me, choosing to call my member of congress has been nothing but a success. First, I submitted a meeting request through my Representative's website explaining that I wanted to discuss my support for HR2408, a bill that advocates for refugee girls having access to an education. I received an email a couple of hours later explaining that my Representative would not be able to meet with me, but a staff member would be glad to have a phone call. The call was quick and easy! I introduced myself, told the staffer a little bit about what I do in relation to activism and advocacy, and why I support HR2408 becoming a law.

The staffer was in total agreement with me and said that my Representative would be glad to co-sponsor the bill, and he did! Basically, when a Representative co-sponsors a bill, they are saying that they support it. When a bill is introduced it needs a high amount of co-sponsors for it to even be considered by the Senate to eventually become a law. My choosing to make a phone call brought the mission one step forward to a refugee girl having an opportunity to an education. If I can make that big of a difference all because of one phone call, **then you can too.**

Refer to the sample call scripts below:

Sample Call Script **(Representative)**

Hello, my name is [Your Name] and I am a [Your Age] year-old student at [Your School]. I am calling today to discuss my concerns about [HR____/ISSUE/BILL THAT YOU SUPPORT OR OPPOSE. [Explain the background of the issue and why it's important to you]. [Use facts and data to back yourself up]

Sample Call Script **(Senator)**

Hello, my name is [Your Name] and I am a [Your Age] year-old student at [Your School]. I am calling today to discuss my concerns about [S____/ISSUE/BILL THAT YOU SUPPORT OR OPPOSE. [Explain the background of the issue and why it's important to you]. [Use facts and data to back yourself up]

Write a Letter or Email your Member of Congress:

A nice handwritten letter is always a thoughtful gesture. An email is also a quick and effective way to send a message to someone. Either way, all you have to do is type or handwrite everything you'd like to say to your Member of Congress. When writing to your Member of Congress here is what you should aim to include in a 3 paragraph letter:

*To your **Senator:***

The Honorable (full name)

(Room #) (Name) Senate Office Building

United States Senate

Washington, DC 20510

Dear Senator (last name):

OR

*To your **Representative:***

The Honorable (full name)

(Room #) (Name) House Office Building

United States House of Representatives

Washington, DC 20515

Dear Representative (last name):

Opening Paragraph - Clearly state your position and why you hold it. Urge the Member of Congress to take specific action (ex. vote for/against a particular bill or amendment; co-sponsor a bill; etc.)

Body Paragraph - Give more information on the bill/action and state evidence supporting your position.

Closing Paragraph - A brief summary and provide final encouragement.

Where to Find Your Member of Congress' Email:

Go to your Member of Congress' government website (ending in .gov) and click the "Contact" button

Where to mail your letter(s):

To Senator:

The Honorable (full name)

(Room #) (Name) Senate Office Building

United States Senate

Washington, DC 20510

To Representative:

The Honorable (full name)

(Room #) (Name) House Office Building

United States House of Representatives

Washington, DC 20515

Set Up A Meeting with your Member of Congress:

You may be thinking, *huh*? Many teens are unaware of the fact that they have as much access to their Members of Congress as any other U.S. Citizen does. Your local Representatives and Senators work for you and your community. That is why they are called public servants. They are here to serve your needs and listen to you voice your concerns. Setting up a meeting with your local Member of Congress is an excellent way to advocate for a bill or cause you support, but if you don't like a certain law or policy then you can also use the meeting to express your anger and dissatisfaction. Here's how you can schedule a meeting with your Senator or Representative:

Plan carefully.

Assemble a small group of constituents (people who live in the same district as you) to attend the meeting with you and agree on one particular issue to address. Try to schedule your meeting during a congressional recess when your representatives are more likely to be home from Washington.

Make an appointment.

Call the legislator's home district office (not the Washington, D.C. office) and ask to schedule a meeting. Be sure to include your name and contact information, note the issue you would like to discuss during the meeting, and suggest a range of times that you can meet.

Prepare.

Agree on a few key talking points and write them down. Find out your legislator's record on the issue you will be addressing. Also, be sure to print out copies of fact sheets that you can share with other attendees during the meeting.

Expect a brief meeting.

Plan to have each participant in your group briefly make one important and unique point during the meeting. Leave time for the legislator or staffer to ask questions and respond to your request for action. Note that meetings with a legislator can be as short as 10–15 minutes, though meetings with legislative staff may last longer.

Be polite, clear and concise.

Tell the legislator or staff member how the issue affects you personally and provide facts and examples to support your argument.

Ask for a specific action.

You have to be specific about what you desire. "Will you sign our pledge to advocate for preventing air pollution?" is a great question that has a specific action. It is okay if the legislator or staffer wants to get back to you later with an answer. That may happen.

Document the meeting.

Make certain that one person in your group takes notes so you can report back to others about what was said. It's also useful to have your camera ready so that you can ask the legislator or staffer to take a picture with the members of your group

Exchange contact information.

Make sure that you get a business card from the person that you meet with. If you have a card, definitely leave it behind.

Follow up after the meeting.

Send a thank-you note for the meeting and watch for your legislator's action on the issue. If a commitment has been made to you, make note of whether there is follow through.

REAL LIFE EXAMPLE: Lobbying is not as hard as you think. Thankfully, I had the opportunity to Lobby on Capitol Hill in Washington D.C. to get some hands on experience. I was in a group of people who all lived in the same state as me and we spent the entire day meeting with the staff of our Senators and Representatives advocating for HR2408. Each person in our group delivered specific talking points and facts to make the meeting run smoothly.

Utilize Online Activism

Over the past few years, I've seen hundreds of activist accounts appear on social media. Although, social media is often filled with funny content and pictures of people's lives, it can also be a powerful tool used for change. With social media, you can share petitions, credible stories to help build awareness on your cause, and more. You could even make an account solely dedicated to your activism.

Create something

In this day and age, creative expressions are a huge influence within activist culture. If you're an artistic person of any kind, get those creative juices flowing and prepare to make a statement. Some examples include, but are not limited to:

- Music
- Art (Painting, Drawing, etc.)
- Dance
- Videography (Documentaries, Short Films, etc.)
- Photography

TEEN ACTIVIST SPOTLIGHT:

Sawyer Taylor-Arnold, 17, says:
I am passionate about equality, especially regarding women's rights and gender equality. This issue is so important in today's society because if half of the population is held back, we aren't reaching our full global potential. Empowering women is critical, and now is the time to do it.

The women who came before us fought for equality on all different levels (gender, racial, economic, etc.) and as young people, it's our job to use our voices to continue this fight. By knowing the struggles and abuse women face every single day around the world, it is our duty to use our platforms to advocate for women who can't advocate for themselves and magnify the voices of those who can.

Growing up, I wasn't aware of a lot of the injustices occurring in the United States, much less around the world. Once I started learning about the struggles many women face I felt I had an obligation to try and create some sort of positive change. Being able to use my voice and advocate for what I'm passionate about has been not only empowering for myself, but empowering for the women who receive the tangible effects of my work.

How Sawyer put her passion into action:

Resisters Co is a small nonprofit that I run to raise money for women in my community and across the globe. I created it when I was 15, during my freshman year of high school with the help of a friend, but now I run it solely. I wanted not only to raise money for this cause, but also to spread an empowering message of unity and activism. Resisters Co was created because I wanted to be able to give back to my community and advocate for things I believe in, while doing something that I enjoy. I design stickers with empowering activist messages and sell them to teenagers at my school and other schools in Western North Carolina.

After over a year and a half, Resisters Co has expanded to an Etsy store. Within the first year of business, we raised over $1,000.00 that went to the local rape and abuse counseling center in my community. Currently, depending on the sticker bought, the funds will go to a different organization based on the message of the sticker.

Connect With Sawyer

Personal Instagram: **@sawyer.taylor.arnold**

Business Instagram: **@resistersco**

Etsy- **ResistersCo**

Volunteer

Volunteering is one of the easiest ways to show your support as an activist. One of the best ways to make a difference is to donate your time to support the mission derived from your passion. Reach out to organizations in your community that do work for your cause, and ask how you can help. If you are interested in supporting animals in need, try volunteering at your local animal shelter or wildlife rescue. If your mission is to end world hunger, then spend a day serving food to people in great need.

Start a Petition

A petition is a formal written request signed by people to appeal to authority for a certain cause. It can be about whatever you would like, and you can address it to whoever you want, whether it be the government, your school, or a company. Just make sure your petition is practical and makes sense. You can make a difference by creating your own petition in just three steps.

Create your goal.

Think about your goal. If you write it down, it may help you. Consider a few questions, such as these:

1) *What do I want to achieve? Is it possible?* **This is the goal of your petition.**

2) *Who can make the change that I am requesting?* **This is your petition target.**

3) *Why should people care about this issue?* **Tell an interesting story.** *Your petition may be important to you, but who else cares?*

Gather and prepare the information.

Before you create your petition, you must have some information ready:

1) Addressee: Do you have the email address of the target of your petition?

2) Data: Do you have enough data and information about the subject and the petition target? This will add validity to your petition. Keep in mind that you know about the problem, but other people may not.

Create the Petition

The most effective method is to use online platforms such as change.org.

Fundraise

Depending on what you're advocating for, fundraising can be very useful. You can give the money you raise to an organization that does the same kind of activism work that you do, but on a larger scale. If you've already decided what you want the money to go towards, that is fine too.

Donate

Oftentimes, we become so wrapped up in the idea of activism consisting of protesting, marching or radical notions, that we forget simply donating money or time to those in need can make a huge difference.

Attend a City Council/Town Hall Meeting

Staying updated on community issues is a must. Before you change the world, you've got to make change within your community first! Attending City Council meetings is a great way to know where your elected representatives stand on issues that matter to you.

Boycott

Boycotting is one of the most popular forms of nonviolent protests. By definition, a boycott is the decision to not use or buy products or services in order to show support for a cause. Is there a company that goes against everything you stand for including your morals, values, and beliefs? Don't buy from there! Your dollar holds more power than you would think and you have the ability to make change just by choosing what companies or businesses you are or aren't willing to support.

REAL LIFE EXAMPLE:

In 1955, one of the largest boycotts to ever occur in American history took place, and that was *the Montgomery Bus Boycott*. Black people in Montgomery, Alabama were fed up with sitting in the back of segregated buses and experiencing brutal racism from White Americans. As a result, they chose to refrain from using the city buses as a way to protest segregation on public transportation. One year later, segregation on public transportation was outlawed and ruled unconstitutional by the U.S. because of a successful boycott.

Intern

If you find a company or organization that is doing work specific to your cause, reach out to them and ask if you can spend a summer interning for them. By doing an internship you'll get hands on experience and learn skills that you can implement within your own life and community to ultimately help achieve the collective goal pertaining to your cause. You can easily do this by submitting an email request.

Hello!

My name is [Your Name] and I am a [Teen Activist/Community Organizer]. I am interested in doing an internship at [Name of Company/Organization] and would like to know if this would be possible. I can be contacted at [Email & Phone Number]

Best Regards, [Your Name]

Join Organizations

Joining organizations that align with your morals, goals, and personal beliefs is a great way to improve yourself as an activist. The key to finding something that would be a good fit for you is to simply do a quick Google search of organizations on the international, national and local scale that cater to what you're interested in. My own real life example, is that I am involved in quite a few organizations that align with my beliefs.

Girl Up (International) - Girl Up is a "for girls, by girls" campaign of the United Nations Foundation that was created to advocate, fundraise, and serve girls in underprivileged countries such as Ethiopia, Guatemala, Liberia, Uganda, and India. Since its launch in 2010, Girl Up has implemented the Teen Advisor program which consists of High School girls who are committed to the empowerment and wellbeing of girls and women. Thankfully, I was one of the 21 girls worldwide to be chosen for the 2017-2018 Class of Teen Advisors. Because of Girl Up, I have been able to connect and form relationships with some amazing girls who have the same passions as me.

You can learn more about how you can get involved at www.GirlUp.org

Black Youth Network (National U.S. Organization) - The Black Youth Network is a non-profit organization that focuses on connecting and empowering young Black leaders who are making positive contributions to the world. We consist of leaders, change-makers, entrepreneurs, scholars, founders and activists who are all passionate about making a difference.

You can learn more about how you can get involved and become a member at www.BlackYouthNetwork.org

LEAD Nation (Local Organization, Florida) – "Leaders by empowerment, Activists by development." LEAD Nation is a community-based nonprofit organization developed to inspire youth to become leaders in their community by providing the necessary training needed for success. The organization focuses on education, mentoring, service, character and public speaking for middle and high school students, as well as provides a platform for parent engagement and learning.

Broward Youth Coalition (Local Organization, Florida) - The Broward Youth Coalition aims to empower youth leaders to advance social change to promote healthy, drug free communities. They empower youth to be change agents, leaders, and promote healthy drug free communities through youth leadership development and education about substance use and abuse.

All of the organizations that I'm a part of align with my personal goals, morals, and beliefs. Being a part of them has not only improved my leadership skills, but has also allowed me to meet like-minded individuals. If you're looking for organizations for youth and student activists that you can be a part of, refer to the "Resources for Student and Youth Activists" chapter towards the end of the book.

As a teenager, the word "organize" can be quite intimidating, but I promise you it's not as scary as you think. You have to come up with effective ways to get your message out which is where being a good organizer comes in handy. Organizing is a great way to sharpen up your leadership skills and educate others on your cause.

Start A Club

Clubs will never go out of style. Whether you're a High School or College student, clubs are a great way for students to participate in activities they enjoy, learn new skills, and meet new people. They can cover a wide variety of topics, from math to animals, protecting the environment, and more.

For school-centered clubs, meetings are usually held before or after school. Some clubs meet regularly and require a large time commitment while others meet once a month or less. Each club usually has a teacher or staff member who acts as a supervisor. Students can hold leadership positions in the club, such as President, Vice-President, and Secretary. Since you'll be the President of your club, you get to choose yourself who you feel would be the best fit for those positions whether you personally elect them or do it democracy style where everyone votes on who gets the position. It's your club, so it's up to you if you're the president.

Many students love participating in clubs because it gives them an opportunity to spend time with their friends and do activities they find fun and interesting. Colleges and employers also like to see students who have participated in extracurricular activities such as clubs, because it helps them understand a student's interests better and it shows that the student likes being involved and working with other people. Before you know it, you'll have hundreds of student activists and your club will be everyone's favorite!

REAL LIFE EXAMPLE:

In August 2017, I started my club *"Girl Up Broward"* which is a county-wide chapter of the United Nation Foundation's Girl Up Campaign. As President of my club, I decided the overall goal and mission for my club would be to empower girls in Broward County, while simultaneously empowering girls in developing countries. My club has monthly meetings, events, and even more!

Here are some effective things that I did and would recommend to anyone interested in starting a club:

1.) Host an interest meeting/info session - This was an opportunity to explain who I was and what the mission/goal of my club was so that people could decide if they wanted to join or not.

2.) Promote on social media - All of my club members that I currently have in my club came from me promoting on social media.

3.) Delegate - Everything should not be done by yourself. You should always aim to split the responsibilities between you and your club members so that everyone feels included and things get done a lot quicker.

Organization

If you really want to take your activism to the next level, you can start an actual organization. This is especially useful if you've already searched for specific types of organizations, but couldn't find what you were looking for. It can be good to take matters into your own hands. The most popular type of organizations that has been started by teenagers are called *non-profits*. These organizations are created without the intention to make profits.

How to Start a Nonprofit Organization as a Teenager:

1. **Choose a cause to support** - Choose the cause that you wish to support which should be in line with your passion. There are thousands of causes that you can support to help make people's lives better.
2. **Decide how you want to support** - As a teenager, you are probably still in school and there may be a limit to the extent to which you can go for your organization. Therefore, you have to decide on what kinds of things you want to do to support your organization.

Some examples include, but are not limited to: collecting used or unwanted clothing around your neighborhood to distribute to people without clothes, gathering some of your old school books, bags, and other educational materials that you and your friends no longer need and giving them out to children who cannot afford to go to school, or offering monetary, moral support, or just help to increase awareness of diseases. The types of things you choose to do in your organization all depends on what your cause is.

3. **Research to expand your knowledge** - To be able to learn more about how to run your organization, you should consider reading books and materials that would give you a deeper insight. You can get a lot of useful books and materials from online book stores like Amazon for less than $10.

4. **Gather a group of like-minded people** - Make your intentions for your organization known to your parents, friends, family, teachers, colleagues at school, and other people that you know. You will need people to support you and your organization, and the only way they will find out is if you spread the word!

5. **Write Your Vision and Mission Statement** -Your vision and statement will make clear what your goals are and what the purpose of your organization is.

Just a Tip: You should strongly consider having some adults that you trust on your Board of Trustees so that they can handle some of the legal responsibilities that you are restricted from doing as a younger teenager. Most restrictions are lifted once you are 18 or 19 years of age.

6. **Appoint a Treasurer** - The Treasurer would take charge of managing the financial responsibilities, such as keeping records of expenses, saving money and keeping all financial records.

7. **Register your Nonprofit Organization as a 501c3** - 501(c)(3) means that a nonprofit organization has been approved by the Internal Revenue Service as a tax-exempt, charitable organization. *"Charitable"* is defined as being established for purposes that are religious, educational, scientific, literary, testing for public safety, fostering of national or international amateur sports, or prevention of cruelty to animals and children. This is one of the reasons why you need an adult on your Board of Trustees so that they would be able to help you register your organization as a not-for-profit organization so that you can be exempted from paying taxes.

8. **Create a website** - Utilize the inexpensive platforms on the internet to create a website for your nonprofit organization. You would be able to reach and help more people when

you have a website. Sponsors can also learn more about your organization and the cause(s) you are supporting through your website.

9. **Raise money** - Since the focus of nonprofits is not to earn money, there are several ways that you can raise funds for your organization:

- Apply for grants from corporate organizations, and other organizations that support charitable causes.
- Organize fundraising events like fashion shows, beauty pageants, and garage sales to raise money.
- Place collection boxes in strategic places so that people can donate to your organization.
- Write letters to corporate organizations for sponsorship.
- Ask for help from your parents and friends or raise money through volunteer work.

Once you have all of these things in place, you can finally start your nonprofit organization. It will definitely be a lot of work, so remember to remain hard-working and remind yourself of your mission and vision statement as a guide to keep you on track.

Awareness Campaign

An awareness campaign is the act of enlightening and informing people of your cause and campaign. When starting an awareness campaign, you should execute a plan that will motivate people to take action. While the obvious goal is to raise awareness about your cause, you have to think about how you will get the largest amount of people involved, which will result in more awareness. For example, if you want to raise awareness about a disease, you can measure that awareness in dollars donated to an organization that researches cures for the disease. That means your goal would be to raise a certain amount of money.

You also have to identify different campaign strategies to use. You might hold a rally in a local park to raise awareness or have volunteers stand on street corners with handmade signs. You can sell products, such as wristbands or T-shirts that advocate your cause. You can even start a social media campaign and create a hashtag that people all over the world can see and use. Don't just focus on one strategy. You want to use different strategies that will appeal to different audiences

Coalition

A coalition is a group of individuals and/or organizations with a common interest who agree to work together toward a collective goal. That goal could be as narrow as obtaining funding for a specific cause, or as broad as trying to permanently improve the overall quality of life for most people in the community. This would be perfect for teens who are not interested in starting their own organizations or awareness campaign, but would rather join with other individuals and organizations.

Plan an Activism Event

From marches, to protests, students and youth have done it all! Planning an event can be very time consuming, but with the help of others it can definitely be done.

Here is how you can plan and host an activism event:

1. **Pick a meaningful topic:** What is your event about? Consider what you are passionate about and what the current events and trending topics are.
2. **Develop a unique approach:** Your event must be creative and unique   to capture people's attention. Think of ways to spread your message in a manner that is unforgettable and cannot be ignored.
3. **Have a team:** When planning anything, especially large events, it is important to have a team of people that can help you manage the responsibilities. *"If you want to go fast go alone. If you want to go far, go together." - African Proverb*
4. **Plan the event:** Make sure everyone in the group understands the purpose of the event, and their role in its success. Make sure

everyone is on the same page so that the event is as successful as possible.

5. **<u>Market the event:</u>** People need to know about your event. Build excitement beforehand so people will want to come check it out, and talk about it afterwards.

6. **<u>Execute the event:</u>** Stay focused, keep your goals in mind, and expect the unexpected.

7. **<u>Follow-up:</u>** The work isn't over when the event ends. Show your appreciation to your volunteers, and celebrate!

STEP 5

KNOW YOUR RIGHTS

As a young activist, you're putting yourself out into the world. That means people are going to be paying attention to you. There are going to be people who support, encourage, and uplift you. There will also be people who don't support you and don't agree with what you're advocating for, because that's just how life is. Everybody isn't rooting for you and there are going to be people who don't want to see you succeeding and changing the world. It is especially important and extremely necessary that you as a teenager know what your rights are. I can guarantee that there will be people who are expecting you to not know a thing about what your rights are simply for the fact that you are young, which is not okay. Prove them wrong!

TEEN ACTIVIST SPOTLIGHT

Khushi Gandhi, 17, says:

"As Teenagers, we often forget how powerful our voice and opinions are. Truth is, they matter. Now more than ever, we need teens to raise their voices to be the disruptive force in society and really bring the change that the world needs."

Although this book is geared towards teens, it is still important to know that in the United States, a minor is someone who's unmarried under the age of 18. The rights of teens 18 and 19-years-old will differ from the ones under 18.

Children are *adequately* protected under the U.S. Constitution, which means only partly protected. Basically, minors have <u>most</u> of the same constitutional rights as adults, but not all. So, here's the answer to the question that's probably in your head right now: Do minors in the United States *really* have rights? To be honest, it's kind of tricky to explain, so I've broken it down into different aspects of the average teen's life where knowing your rights is not only essential, but vital to your overall wellbeing.

Know Your Rights in School

In the United States, you have a right to an education. Young people have to go to school. **Compulsory Attendance** means that until you reach a certain age, it's illegal for you to not be in school. If you skip school, you can be found truant, which is a legal way of saying you're not where you're supposed to be when you should be at school.

School Discipline

Suspension is a form of school discipline which temporarily removes you from a class or from school. Your school may prohibit you from school grounds, a classroom, or place you in a supervised (in-school) suspension classroom that is separate from other students.

Before your school can suspend you they must try other interventions to change your behavior. They should only result to suspension after interventions fail, unless your behavior is very serious, violent, or dangerous to others.

During the process of suspension you have the right to an informal pre-suspension conference with school or district staff, unless there is an emergency situation that results in automatic suspension. You should be able to tell your side of the story and present evidence in the conference before they decide if you should be suspended or not.

Expulsion is the removal or banning of a student from a school system for an extensive period of time due to a student continuously violating the school's rules, or for a single offense in extreme cases that differ depending on the school district. Some extreme actions that will result in expulsion includes: possessing or selling firearms, threatening another person with a knife, selling drugs, attempting or committing a sexual assault, possessing an explosive, or inflicting serious bodily harm on someone.

Before your school can expel you, they must:

- *Give you the right to request an expulsion hearing.* Before your hearing, your school district must continue to offer you an educational program. Your school district will make the final expulsion decision at your hearing.
- *Provide you with written notice of your expulsion hearing date* at lea-st ten days prior to your hearing.
- *Allow you to access your student records* and inspect evidence to be used against you before your expulsion hearing, if you choose to do so.

During the process of expulsion, you have the right to:

- Bring advocates to help tell your side of the story.
- Request a written final decision, and the right to an appeal.

If you win your hearing, you usually return back to your school immediately. If you don't, you should check with your school district to see if you will be eligible to return to your school district after expulsion.

Corporal Punishment

School corporal punishment is the act of causing deliberate pain or discomfort in response to undesired behavior by students in schools. It often involves "spanking" the student either across the bottom or on the hands, with items such as: a wooden paddle, slipper, leather strap, or wooden yardstick.

It is currently legal and illegal in the following states:

Legal

Alabama, Arizona, Arkansas, Colorado, Florida, Georgia, Idaho, Indiana, Kansas, Kentucky, Louisiana, Mississippi, Missouri, North Carolina, Oklahoma, South Carolina, Tennessee, Texas, and Wyoming.

Illegal

Alaska, California, Connecticut, Delaware, District of Columbia, Hawaii, Illinois, Iowa, Maine, Maryland, Massachusetts, Michigan, Minnesota, Montana, Nebraska, Nevada, New Hampshire, New Jersey, New Mexico, New York North Dakota Ohio, Oregon, Pennsylvania, Rhode Island, South Dakota, Utah, Vermont, Virginia, Washington, West Virginia, and Wisconsin.

Permission to use corporal punishment in the states where it is allowed is determined by each school district. If a school district permits corporal punishment, it still must follow federal and state law concerning physical contact between adults and children.

If you feel that you or someone you know has been the victim of excessive physical contact with a school official, you should tell your parents and report this situation to your principal and superintendent as soon as possible. Some school districts also may include waivers that your parents can sign preventing corporal punishment. If you and your parents feel strongly against this issue, you should contact your school district to discuss this option.

Privacy

You have a right to privacy and confidentiality in school. The 1974 law called the Family Educational Rights and Privacy

Act, or FERPA, states that your school records including grades and personal information is a private thing. Until you turn 18, only your parents will have access to your confidential info.

Personal Records

Keeping your business private is an important right. There is some information that's still public, like your name, address, and date of birth. It's a good idea to check this out with your school so you know what they consider public and what they keep private.

In some situations, your school records become public. Anything involving the police or law enforcement becomes a public issue. For example, if you are involved in a physical altercation and the police are called in, your school records can become public information. The police report is open to anyone who wants to read it. Your records can also be requested by the court. If that happens, the school can give the court your information without your permission.

Student Searches

In a public high school the right to be free from an unwarranted search is dramatically reduced. School authorities need less suspicion of wrong-doing and must adhere to a less restrictive "reasonable suspicion" standard to search you. That means if school officials suspect you of having broken a school rule, they may search you and your property to attempt to confirm or disprove that suspicion.

Drug Tests

Suspicion about an individual student's possible drug use must be reasonable before school officials require that child to take a drug test.

Students with Disabilities

Playing Sports

The Rehabilitation Act of 1973, a law that prohibits discrimination on the basis of disability, requires that students with disabilities be provided equal opportunity for participation in interscholastic, club, and intramural athletics programs offered or sponsored by a school.

Bullying/Harassment

Unfortunately, students with disabilities are much more likely to be bullied than their non-disabled peers. According to the U.S. Department of Education, schools must address bullying and harassment that are based on a student's disability and that interfere with or limit a student's ability to participate in or benefit from the services, activities, or opportunities offered by a school.

Undocumented Immigrant Students

Undocumented students are school-aged immigrants who entered the United States without inspection or overstayed their visas and are present in the United States with or without their parents. They face unique challenges and limitations within the United States educational system.

Enrolling in Public School (K-12)

In the 1982 Plyer v. Doe 457 US 202 case, the United States Supreme Court ruled that undocumented children living in the United States could not be excluded from public elementary and secondary schools based upon their immigration status. This means that immigrant students are allowed to enroll in public school no matter their immigration status.

U.S. Immigration and Customs Enforcement (ICE) at School

The Family Educational Rights and Privacy Act (FERPA) does not allow schools to turn over a student's file to federal immigration agents.

Applying to College

There is no federal or state law that prohibits the admission of undocumented immigrants to U.S. colleges. Federal or state laws do not require students to prove citizenship in order to enter

U.S. institutions of higher education, however individual states may admit or bar undocumented students from enrolling as a matter of policy or through legislation. Many states do not prohibit the admission of undocumented students to public institutions, while private universities are free to admit undocumented students regardless of state laws.

Tips for Undocumented Students When Applying To College:

- **Ask admission offices how your immigration status will affect the college application process.**

Students should contact every school they plan to apply to learn how their application will be treated as an undocumented student.

- **Work with college access programs while in high school.**

College access programs can help with various things such as standardized test prep, helping students find or apply for scholarships, and more. To find a college access program in your area, ask a teacher, local college, or try your local YMCA chapter.

- **Consider the campus environment.**

Think about what the school's community has to offer in terms of a positive social climate and services for undocumented students.

- **Look for private scholarships while in high school.** The ideal time to start looking for scholarships is early in your junior year of high school, or even before that. For undocumented students, private scholarships can offer important coverage for discretionary costs like meals, housing, transportation and books in addition to covering your tuition.

- **Ask colleges if you qualify for institutional aid.** Undocumented students are not eligible for federal financial aid such as Federal Pell Grants, Federal Work-Study, and Federal Direct Student Loans (Direct Loans). However, they may be eligible for financial aid from other sources, including from the college and private organizations.

LGBTQ+ Students

Lesbian, Gay, Bisexual, and Transgender students often face discrimination and harassment while at school. If you're in one of those categories or know someone who is, it is important to know what to do if someone isn't being treated fairly.

Harassment

If you are getting bullied, harassed, or threatened because of your sexuality or gender identity, report it to your counselor or

Principal immediately. Title IX, a federal education law, prevents public schools from ignoring harassment based on gender stereotyping.

Privacy

Your school doesn't have the right to "out" your sexuality without your permission. Every student has a Constitutional right to privacy.

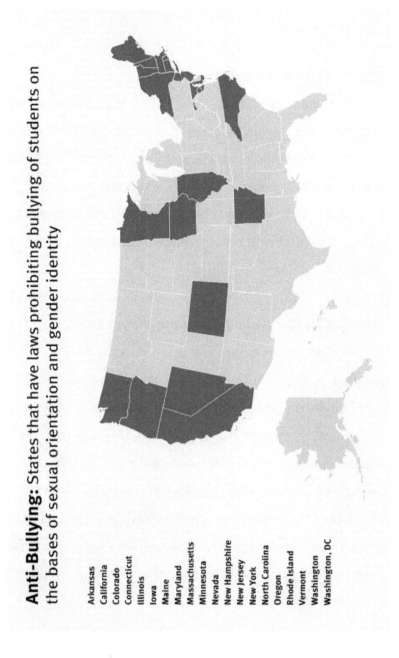

Anti-Bullying: States that have laws prohibiting bullying of students on the bases of sexual orientation and gender identity

Arkansas
California
Colorado
Connecticut
Illinois
Iowa
Maine
Maryland
Massachusetts
Minnesota
Nevada
New Hampshire
New Jersey
New York
North Carolina
Oregon
Rhode Island
Vermont
Washington
Washington, DC

Image: www.hrw.org/report/2016/12/07/walking-through-hailstorm/discrimination-against-lgbt-youth-us-schools

Expressing Your Sexuality

Oftentimes, schools will try to silence students who are open about their sexual orientation. You have a Constitutional right to be "out of the closet" at school if you choose to be. For example, wearing LGBTQ positive t-shirts, stickers and bracelets, is completely okay. The only time your school can legally restrict your speech is when it causes significant disruption in the classroom.

Transgender and Gender Non-Conforming Students

Your gender expression is protected by the U.S. constitution and Title IX. This includes wearing your choice of clothes even if it isn't stereotypically associated with your gender. Unfortunately, there aren't yet clear standards and rules on how schools should accommodate transgender and gender non-conforming students when it comes to restrooms, locker rooms, use of names/pronouns and how your official school records will classify you. However, it is completely okay for you to politely ask if others would call you by your chosen name and pronouns if that is what you choose to do.

School Dances and other events

The First Amendment and your right to equal protection guarantees you the right to express yourself, so you should be able to bring a same-sex date to the prom, homecoming, or any school dances/events if you choose.

Conversion Therapy

Conversion therapy sometimes known as "reparative therapy," is a range of dangerous and discredited practices that falsely claim to change a person's sexual orientation or gender identity. Conversion Therapy specifically discriminates against LGBTQ+ people, because it is designed to change one's sexual orientation or gender identity.

Conversion Therapy often consists of extreme practices such as:

- Electric Shocking
- Harassment
- Physical Abuse
- Mental Abuse

Which can lead to...

- Suicide
- Depression
- Self-Hate

If a teacher, or school staff member recommends or tries to perform conversion therapy to an LGBTQ+ student, tell someone immediately.

Gay Straight Alliances/ Gender & Sexuality Alliances

GSAs are made up of students of any sexual orientation or gender identity, not just gay students. They can serve as support groups, social groups, or a combination of both. The Equal Access Act allows students to form or create GSA's at their school, just like any other club.

Pregnant and Parenting Students

In October 2009, approximately 3 million 16-through 24-year-olds living in the United States were not enrolled in high school and had not earned a high school diploma or alternative credential. Students give a range of reasons for dropping out of high school, both school-and family-related. Pregnancy was the most common family related reason given by female students according to the U.S. Department of Education.

Classes and School Activities

According to Title IX, a law that was enacted in 1972, it is illegal to exclude pregnant and parenting students from school. Your School must:

- Allow you to continue participating in classes and extracurricular activities even though you are pregnant. This means that you can still participate in advanced placement and honors classes, school clubs, sports, honor societies, student leadership opportunities, and other activities, like after-school programs operated at the school.

- Allow you to choose whether you want to participate in special instructional programs or classes for pregnant students. You can participate if you want to, but your school cannot pressure you to do so. The alternative program must provide the same types of academic, extracurricular and enrichment opportunities as your school's regular program.

- Provide you with reasonable adjustments, like a larger desk, elevator access, or allowing you to make frequent trips to the restroom, when necessary because of your pregnancy.

Harassment

According to the Office of Civil Rights of the U.S. Department of Education your school <u>must</u> protect you from harassment based on sex, including harassment because of pregnancy or related conditions. Comments that could constitute prohibited harassment include making sexual comments or jokes about a student's pregnancy, calling someone sexually charged names, spreading rumors about sexual activity, and making sexual propositions or gestures, when the comments are sufficiently serious and interfere with your ability to benefit from or participate in school.

Absences and Medical Leave

The Office of Civil Rights under the U.S. Department of Education exclaims that Title IX requires a school to excuse a student's absences due to pregnancy or related conditions, including recovery from childbirth, so your school must do the following things:

- Excuse absences due to pregnancy or childbirth for as long as your doctor says it is necessary.
- Allow you to return to the same academic and extracurricular status as before your medical leave began, which should include giving you the opportunity to make up any work missed while you were out.
- Your teacher may not refuse to allow you to submit work after a deadline you missed because of pregnancy or childbirth. If your teacher's grading is based in part on class participation or attendance and you missed class because of pregnancy or childbirth, you should be allowed to make up the participation or attendance credits you didn't have the chance to earn.
- Provide pregnant students with the same special services it provides to students with temporary medical conditions.

This includes homebound instruction/at-home tutoring/independent study.

Breastfeeding

Students who are pregnant or parenting should be provided a comfortable space to breastfeed or pump milk.

Students of Color

With rising racial tensions in America, students of color often fear for their safety at school. In many cases, students are experiencing racism, harassment, and they don't know what to do. Here are some words that are going to be used which you should have a clear understanding of:

Prejudice – A preconceived **opinion** that is not based on reason or actual experiences.

Racism – Many people were taught that racism is simply disliking someone because of the color of their skin, and that anyone can experience it. Before you believe what people have told you, here is a short recap on the history and invention of Racism.

Racism is an ideology that originated from White European scientists in the 17th Century during the Trans-Atlantic slave trade.

The construct of race was <u>created</u> so that White Europeans could differentiate themselves from those with different skin colors, ultimately creating a system of racial hierarchy in which anyone who did not belong to the White race could not benefit from such a system that still exists to this day. That is why I specifically and intentionally titled this section *"Students of Color"*.

*Prejudice and Racism are **<u>NOT</u>** the same things. To clarify, racism, is a *system* and prejudice is based off of *opinions*. The two words are **<u>NOT</u>** interchangeable.

Hate Crimes at School

The term "hate crime" refers to an attack on an individual or his or her property (e.g., vandalism, arson, assault, murder) in which the victim is intentionally selected because of their race, color, religion, national origin, gender, disability, or sexual orientation.

Sample Scenario & Example

Amala is a student at Sunny Tree High School. She practices Islam and has recently decided to start wearing a hijab. She says that wearing her hijab makes her feel empowered and proud to be a Muslim. One day, Amala came to school only to find the word **terrorist** written in large red letters on her locker. She was heartbroken that someone would call her such a terrible word that was not true. She decided to tell the principal immediately and was told that they would figure out who did it immediately. A couple of hours later, Amala is sitting in her History class when she hears a group of white male students behind her whispering the word **'terrorist'**. She decides to just ignore them, until one of them pulls her hijab off of her head. She then gets extremely angry and yells at them to give her the hijab back.

What Amala has experienced in this scenario is an example of a hate crime.

What to Do

If you have witnessed or have been a victim of a hate crime at school you should tell a teacher or guidance counselor immediately. If they do not take action, you should tell the principal of your school or contact the Superintendent of your school district. You can also file a discrimination complaint with the Office for Civil Rights of the U.S. Department of Education.

Religious Students

Freedom of religion means the government may not establish or encourage any single religion, nor may the government limit your freedom to practice any religion. This is stated in the First Amendment of the U.S. Constitution. This means that even when you are at school, your freedom to practice your religion does not go away.

Religious Wear

The First Amendment allows for mandatory uniform policies or dress codes in U.S. public schools. However, it also generally permits exemptions from such policies or codes for students to wear religious garb, head coverings, symbols or other attire.

Student Prayers

Religious Students have the right to pray individually or in groups or to discuss their religious views with peers as long as it is not disruptive. For Example: If a teacher calls on you to answer a question, you shouldn't just start praying out of nowhere.

Starting a Religious-based Club

The Equal Access Act requires public secondary schools which meet certain criteria to treat all student-initiated groups equally, regardless of the religious, political, philosophical or other orientation of the groups.

Religious Dietary Restrictions

Schools are not required to adhere to dietary restrictions due to religious reasons, but in most cases, students can bring their own lunch to school.

Social Media Use

The average teenager spends over an hour a day on social media. It has become such a big part of society that many teenagers, including me, couldn't imagine life without it! Social media includes apps and websites like Facebook, Instagram, Snapchat, and Twitter **to name a few.**

Using social media at school

You have a constitutional right to free speech and the right to express your opinions and beliefs, even if they are controversial, as long as you do so in a way that doesn't disrupt class or other school-related activities. *However*, most schools have internet and phone usage policies. If you are using a school computer or email account, school officials <u>can</u> monitor your activity. Any online activity using school computers, internet access, or email accounts that violate school policies, creates a disruptive learning environment, or violates others' rights could result in consequences.

Using Social Media Outside Of School

Depending on what you post, you can get in trouble for certain types of social media usage outside of school such as cyberbullying or harassment on the basis of sex, religion, and/or race.

Scenario: A 17-year-old Junior named Sarah posts a racist message toward her Black classmates threatening to harm them at school the next day on her social media. The next thing you know, word spreads and the screenshot of Sarah's nasty message spreads and lands in the hands of the school Principal. Sarah then gets suspended for 2 days. Is this an acceptable consequence for Sarah's actions?

Answer: Yes, this was an acceptable consequence because Sarah's behavior outside of school directly and substantially disrupts the school.

Military Recruiting

Military Recruiting is the act of attracting people to, and selecting them for, military training and employment. Oftentimes, going to the military is over glamorized which is what tends to attract teenagers. They are told that they are making a good choice by dedicating themselves to "serve the country". What many teenagers don't realize is that choosing to enlist in the military is a huge life choice and can involve extreme levels of violence that may result in death or psychological issues such as Post Traumatic Stress Disorder (PTSD). Low income students, immigrant students, and students of color are especially targeted for military recruiting. Whatever your stance on military recruiting may be, here is what you need to know:

Your personal information in the hands of the military

Unfortunately, your school district can send your personal information to military recruiters without your consent. Under the No Child Left Behind Act, if a military recruiter asks your school for student contact information (name, address, phone numbers) and the student or parent has not notified the school that they want this information kept private, the school must hand over the information.

Opting out

If you do not want military recruiters to have access to your personal information, you or your parent needs to request to your school in writing that you want your personal information kept private. Before schools turn your information over to military recruiters, they must notify you of this option.

Junior Reserve Officer Training Corps (JROTC)

Junior Reserve Officer Training Corps is a U.S. military-run program for high school students. JROTC is taught by retired military personnel and involves classroom work combined with a · military curriculum. Although students who participate in JROTC may wear military uniforms, they are not in the military.

Your school cannot force you to join the JROTC. The classes are strictly voluntary. If you choose to join the JROTC, you do not have to further your commitment or feel pressured to join the military.

Sexual Harassment

Sexual harassment can be defined as requests for sexual favors or unwelcomed sexual behavior that makes you feel uncomfortable, scared or confused and that interferes with your schoolwork or your ability to participate in extracurricular activities or attend classes. Sexual harassment can be verbal (comments about your body, spreading sexual rumors, sexual remarks or accusations, dirty jokes or stories), physical (grabbing, rubbing, flashing or mooning, touching, pinching in a sexual way, sexual assault) or visual (display of naked pictures or obscene gestures). Sexual harassment can happen to people of all gender identities. Sexual harassers can be students, teachers, principals, janitors, coaches, and other school officials.

Sexual harassment is a serious problem for students at all educational levels. This problem is more common than you might think because many students are scared or too embarrassed to report sexual harassment.

Sample Sexual Harassment Scenarios

1) Jane Doe is a student in Mr. Green's Math class. Mr. Green is known as everyone's favorite teacher, but he has started doing things that makes Jane feel uncomfortable. He asks her to come to his room alone after school to discuss her schoolwork. When she shows up, he only talks about how pretty she is and he has put his hand on her thigh a couple of times. He also always asks for a hug before she leaves. He is now suggesting that they have their afterschool meetings at a café in the city. He tells her that she must continue to attend these meetings if she wants to earn a good grade in his class.

2) John is constantly getting attention from a particular girl in his high school. She sends him sexually explicit notes and blows kisses at him, she even waits for John when he gets off the school bus and when he gets out of class. Someone keeps calling his house, asking for him, and then hanging up, and John is sure it's the girl. He

has even seen her drive by his house in the evening. At first, John thought it was just "flirting", but as the sexual gestures got worse, it started to embarrass and frustrate him. It got to the point where John started to avoid going out so he didn't have to run into the girl; along with him pretending to be sick a few times so he didn't have to go to school.

When unwanted touching, comments, and/or gestures because of your sex are so bad or occur so often that it interferes with your schoolwork, makes you feel uncomfortable or unsafe at school, or prevents you from participating in or benefiting from a school program or activity, this is called hostile environment harassment.

What to do if you are being sexually harassed at school

Sexual harassment is a serious issue that should not be taken lightly. Many students who have been sexually harassed report a drop in their grades, and some students have even had to transfer to a different school, drop classes, or leave school altogether.

IMPORTANT

Here are some things you and/or your parents can do:

- ***Don't blame yourself.*** The person who is harassing you is the one doing   something wrong.
- ***Say "No" Clearly.*** Tell the person who is harassing you that his/her behavior is unacceptable and makes you feel uncomfortable. They may not realize how hurtful they are being and may need a clear message from you to stop.
- ***Write down what happened.*** When someone harasses you or makes you feel uncomfortable, write it down in a notebook that is just for that purpose. Write down what happened, the date it occurred, where it took place, and who else may have witnessed or heard the harassment. Also write down what you did in response, and how the

harassment made you feel. Do not write other information in this notebook, such as to-do lists or homework assignments.

- **Report the Harassment.** It is very important that you tell your parents or another adult, like a teacher or guidance counselor, about the harassment. If you want the school to do something about the harassment, you **MUST** tell a school official, such as the principal, that you are being sexually harassed. If you do not feel comfortable telling the school official yourself, get the help of your parents, a teacher, guidance counselor or another adult to go with you. If you and/or your parents tell a school official verbally, also do it in writing and keep a copy for yourself. If the first school official (like the principal) doesn't take action, go to the school board or Superintendent to complain. There are laws that say the school has to stop the sexual harassment of a student whether the harasser is a teacher or another student(s), but the school is only required to stop the harassment if someone in authority at the school knows what is happening to you. It is **VERY IMPORTANT** to report the harassment to a school official.

- **Consult the school grievance policies and Title IX officer.** Your school is supposed to have a policy against sexual harassment. The Title IX grievance policy may also give you a list of the types of behavior that the school considers to be sexual harassment. Find out from your school who the Title IX officer or coordinator is for your school or district. You should be able to ask them questions about how to complain, and what to expect during the complaint and investigation process.

- *File a Complaint With a Government Agency.* If nothing happens after complaining to school officials, you and/or your parents can file a complaint against the school with the U.S. Department of Education's Office of Civil Rights (OCR). Generally, you must file a complaint with the OCR within 180 days of an act of discrimination or harassment. You can call them, and they will explain to you how to file a complaint.

Office of Civil Rights, U.S. Department of Education

The federal agency that enforces school sexual harassment laws (800) 421-3481: National toll-free hotline to report any educational discrimination, to request information on civil rights compliance programs and procedures for filing discrimination complaints.

Pledge of Allegiance & Patriotism, and more

Standing for and reciting the Pledge of Allegiance + Saluting the Flag

The 1943 Supreme Court Case, West Virginia State Board of Education v. Barnette, 319 U.S. 624 ruled that the Free Speech Clause of the First Amendment protects students from being forced to salute the American flag or say the Pledge of Allegiance in public schools. You cannot be forced to take oaths you do not believe. You cannot be punished by your school for refusing to salute the flag, say the Pledge of Allegiance, or rise while others say the Pledge. You also cannot be required to leave the room when others are saluting the flag if you choose not to. You should maintain a respectful silence while others recite the Pledge. You do not have to give your teacher or other school staff a reason for not participating and you do not need your parent's permission to exercise the right of conscience to refrain from reciting the Pledge. The same conditions apply to standing for, taking a knee, or reciting the National Anthem (Star Spangled Banner)

REAL LIFE EXAMPLE

Personally, I do not embody an ounce of patriotism. The feeling of being patriotic is completely foreign to me. It is not a representation of who I am, so I won't force myself to feel like that's what I "should" be.

I remember being in the 8th grade and deciding that I would no longer say the Pledge of Allegiance. As a Black teenager, I didn't feel that the words "liberty and justice for all" applied to me due to all of the injustices I witnessed. Although I was thirteen at the time of that decision, I still feel the same way to this day.

Everybody in my class performed the same routine every single day: the morning announcements would come on, followed by the Pledge of Allegiance, and everyone would place their hand on their heart to recite the lyrics of the song in synchronicity while I stood there in silence. Throughout the school year, no one ever asked me why I didn't say the Pledge, but they did give me looks. Looks that screamed, "What is wrong with you?" and "Why aren't you saying the Pledge?!" I must admit that it did bother me at first. Sometimes I thought to myself, "Am I making the right choice?" Overall, I did not let the looks get to me and I continued to stand firm in my beliefs.

Protesting at School

The right to protest is a fundamental right protected by the Constitution. However, this does not mean you can protest whenever and wherever you want. Schools have the obligation of creating a learning environment and protests cannot disrupt it. For example, you might not be able to have a protest that blocks the front door to your school, or one that prevents students from reaching their classrooms. You also can be disciplined for cutting class to attend a protest.

Know Your Rights At Home

Some people have excellent parents and others have not-so-good parents. Regardless of how your parents are, it is still extremely important for minors to know what your rights are at home.

Responsibilities of Your Parents

Your parents are legally required to support you which includes providing food, clothing, shelter, and basic care. If your parents fail to provide you with the basic legal requirements, that is called child neglect and abuse.

Types of Child Neglect:

- *Physical neglect* involves the failure of a caregiver to provide for the basic physical needs of a child, such as food, shelter, clothing, and sanitary living conditions. A parent can also be found guilty of neglect if they abandon their child.

- *Educational neglect* occurs when parents don't enroll the child in school or an alternative educational method such as home-schooling.
- *Psychological/emotional neglect* includes a wide variety of behaviors, such as humiliation, insult, having a lack of affection, ignoring the child's basic attention needs, and threatening serious punishment.
- *Medical neglect* is when a parent fails to provide their child with needed medical care.

What to Do

If you are experiencing or are a witness to neglect, report to your local child services authority immediately. You can also contact The Childhelp National Child Abuse Hotline at 1-800-422-4453 or 1-800-4-A-CHILD. The hotline serves the U.S. and Canada, and is staffed 24 hours a day, 7 days a week with professional crisis counselors who provide assistance in over 170 languages. All calls are kept confidential.

Emancipation

Emancipation is the court process through which a minor becomes a legal adult responsible for his or her own care. How do you know if you're really ready for emancipation? Well, here are some things that the court will consider:

Money – Can you support yourself currently or in the future without illegal activities or welfare?

**Where you are living?** – Are you currently living apart from your parents or have you made adequate arrangements if you are granted emancipation?

**Decision Making** – Can you adequately make good decisions for yourself?

**Maturity** – Are you mature enough to function as an adult?

**Education** – Are you attending school or have you already received a diploma?

**Pregnancy** – If you are pregnant, how do you plan to care for yourself and your baby?

Know Your Rights at Work

If you are a working teen, there are federal and state restrictions on what kinds of things you can do at work that were designed to keep you safe.

Where teens can work:

If you are under 14 you are only allowed to:

- deliver newspapers to customers;
- babysit on a casual basis;
- work as an actor or performer in movies, TV, radio, or theater;

- work as a homeworker gathering evergreens and making evergreen wreaths; and

- work for a business owned entirely by your parents as long as it is not in mining, manufacturing, or any of the 17 hazardous occupations.

If you are 14 or 15 you are allowed to do:

- retail occupations;

- intellectual or creative work such as computer programming, teaching, tutoring, singing, acting, or playing an instrument;

- errands or delivery work by foot, bicycle and public transportation;

- clean-up and yard work which does not include using power-driven mowers, cutters, trimmers, edgers, or similar equipment;

- work in connection with cars and trucks such as dispensing gasoline or oil and washing or hand polishing;

- some kitchen and food service work including reheating food, washing dishes, cleaning equipment, and limited cooking;

- cleaning vegetables and fruits, wrapping sealing, labeling, weighing, pricing, and stocking of items when performed in areas separate from a freezer or meat cooler;

- loading or unloading objects for use at a worksite including rakes, hand-held clippers, and shovels;
- 14 and 15-year-olds who meet certain requirements can perform limited tasks in sawmills and wood-shops; and
- 15-year-olds who meet certain requirements can perform lifeguard duties at traditional swimming pools and water amusement parks.

If an occupation is not specifically permitted, it is prohibited for youth ages 14 and 15.

If you are 16 or 17 you are allowed to work any job that has not been declared hazardous by the Secretary of Labor.

Anyone under 18 __CANNOT__ work in the following hazardous occupations:

- Manufacturing or storing of explosives;
- Driving a motor vehicle or working as an outside helper on motor vehicles (More information on Hazardous Occupation #2, driving on the job and Distracted Driving);
- Coal mining;
- Forest fire fighting and forest fire prevention, timber tract, forestry service, and occupations in logging and saw-milling;

- Using power-driven woodworking machines (More information on woodworking);
- Exposure to radioactive substances and ionizing radiation;
- Using power-driven hoisting apparatus;
- Using power-driven metal-forming, punching and shearing machines;
- Mining, other than coal;
- Using power-driven meat-processing machines, slaughtering, meat and poultry packing, processing, or rendering;
- Using power-driven bakery machines;
- Using balers, compactors, and power-driven paper-products machines (More information on using balers, compactors, and paper-products machines);
- Manufacturing brick, tile, and related products;
- Using power-driven circular saws, band saws, guillotine shears, chain saws, reciprocating saws, wood chippers, and abrasive cutting discs (More information on power tools);
- Working in wrecking, demolition, and ship-breaking operations;
- Roofing and work performed on or about a roof (More information on roofing);
- Trenching or excavating.

Once you turn 18, you can perform any job.

Child Labor Laws
If you are 14 or 15:

All work must be performed outside school hours and you may not work:

- more than 3 hours on a school day, including Friday;
- more than 18 hours per week when school is in session;
- more than 8 hours per day when school is not in session;
- more than 40 hours per week when school is not in session; and before 7 a.m. or after 7 p.m. on any day, except from June 1st through Labor Day, when nighttime work hours are extended to 9 p.m.

If you are home schooled, attend private school, or no school, a "school day" or "school week" is any day or week when the public school where you live while employed is in session. There are some exceptions to the hour's standards for 14 and 15-year-olds: if you have graduated from high school, you are excused from compulsory school attendance, or you are enrolled in an approved Work Experience, Career Exploration Program or Work-Study Program.

If you are 16 or 17 you may work unlimited hours.

If you are 18 there are no limits to the number of hours you can work.

Wages

The federal minimum wage is currently $7.25 per hour. However, the youth minimum wage of $4.25 per hour applies to employees under the age of 20 during their first 90 consecutive calendar days of employment with an employer. After 90 days, the Fair Labor Standards Act (FLSA) requires employers to pay the full federal minimum wage.

Know Your Rights in the Court System/with Law Enforcement

Interacting with the Police

If you ever find yourself in a situation with the police, you should know your rights and feel empowered to assert them.

Levels of Interactions with Police Officers

1. Conversation

You are not obligated to speak to the police, an investigator, or anyone except a judge. If you agree to talk to the police, be careful. You might give them information that they could use to arrest you or someone else. If you <u>do not</u> want to talk to the police, the best thing for you to do is too politely, but firmly, refuse to speak to them.

Sample Conversation

Police Officer: "Hi, can I ask you a couple of questions?"

You: "Are you detaining me or am I free to go?"

*This is **VERY** important for you to remember!*

Police Officer: I would just like to talk to you.

You: I choose not to talk to you.

Tricks that police officers may use to get your cooperation:

"If you tell the truth, you can go home."

"You can tell me the truth. You don't need an attorney."

"If you tell me what your friends did, nothing will happen to you."

If a Police Officer makes promises to you, chances are, you won't be able to enforce them later. They are allowed to lie and they are not obligated to tell you the truth. If you aren't sure of what to do, always ask for an attorney before you answer any questions.

2. Detention

Police officers are only <u>supposed</u> to detain you if they have a reasonable suspicion that you are involved in a crime, but unfortunately that isn't the case in many situations.

If you are stopped by the police:

- Try to stay calm and have as much control over your words and actions as you possibly can. You should avoid arguing with the police, but be sure to firmly assert your rights.
- Try your best not to run or physically resist the police. There is a chance that doing so could make the situation drastically worse. Even if you do not resist, they can still say that you did, so it is just better not to.
- Ask: "Am I free to leave?" If they say yes, then leave. Always remember that you are not required to provide identification unless you are the driver of a car.

What to do if you are being detained:

- You must provide your name, address, and date of birth if you are detained, but you are not required to state anything else.
- Ask why you are being detained. They do not have to respond back to you, but if they do give an answer, be sure to memorize it.

Write down everything you can possibly remember about your interactions with the Police including the <u>name(s)</u> and <u>badge number(s)</u> of the Officer(s) when you have the chance.

Sample Conversation

Officer: "Hi, can I ask you a couple of questions?"

You: "Are you detaining me or am I free to go?"

Officer: "I'm detaining you. Put your hands against the wall and spread your legs."

You: "Why am I being detained? What is your reasonable suspicion?"

If there is an answer, memorize it.

3. Arrest

- The police officer is only <u>supposed</u> to physically move you, when you are under arrest.

- If you are arrested, ask for a lawyer or your parents immediately. Do not answer any questions from the police until your lawyer or parent arrives. The police are supposed to contact your parent or an adult family member to tell them that you have been arrested.

Sample Conversation

Officer: "I'm placing you under arrest."

You: "I am going to remain silent. I want to contact an attorney."
Once you say these words, the police are legally required to stop questioning you, but that doesn't mean that they will.
Officer: "You will contact your attorney at the police station."
(Hypothetical answer) They may not say this at all.

Know Your Rights in Court

Navigating the juvenile justice system can be scary and confusing, even if you know you haven't done anything wrong or illegal. It's normal to feel powerless and scared around police, lawyers, and judges when you don't know what to do or say. This is why it's important to know what legal rights you have.

Right to a Trial

A trial is a coming together of parties to a dispute, to present information. You should not feel pressured to plead guilty, even if you are told that you will be able to go home sooner. Take time to decide, because this choice will affect the rest of your life. A guilty plea could mean you will go to jail or be on probation for years. If you have a trial, you could be found not guilty.

Speaking in Court

What you say can or may be used against you, so if you don't understand something, ask your lawyer or the judge

BEFORE you leave court. If you still don't understand, ask again, and keep asking until you get the information you need to fully comprehend everything. Remember to be respectful when you speak to the judge and others in court. You will call the judge "Your Honor."

Write Everything Down

You should write everything down or ask a family member to help you keep track of the names of police officers, your lawyer, probation officer and the judge. Get phone numbers, too. Keep all notes and all letters about court dates or probation rules in a safe place, where you can find them.

Know Who's in the Courtroom

The Judge

The judge is in charge of the courtroom. They listen to the information from your probation officer, lawyers, witnesses, and you. Based on the evidence, the judge will decide if you are guilty or not guilty and that determines if there will be a sentencing.

The State Attorney

The state's attorney represents the people of whatever state you are in. The state's attorney's job is to prove that charges against you are true. To do this, they present evidence and witnesses against you.

Defense Lawyer or Public Defender

The defense lawyer works for you. Their job is to tell you about the law, your choices, and to present evidence and witnesses to help you. If you cannot afford to pay for a private lawyer, the court will appoint a lawyer called a public defender for free.

Probation Officer

The probation officer learns about your needs, sets up services for you, gives information to the judge, and supervises you while you are on probation.

Clerk

The clerk is seated next to the judge. They are responsible for all legal records and information about the cases before the judge.

Deputy Sheriff

A deputy sheriff is assigned to each courtroom to keep order and security in the courtroom.

Sentencing

If the judge rules that you are not guilty, then the case is over and you get to go home. If the Judge decides that you are guilty you could be sentenced to:

- Probation
- Receive counseling and/or treatment
- Serve time in a juvenile detention center

Know Your State's Laws

Each state in the U.S. has different laws, which can be different from Federal Laws, the kinds of laws that apply to the entire country. Here some different ways for you to learn your state's laws:

Libraries

These are great places to get started. All you need to do is go to the library and ask for a librarian to point you in the direction of where you can find information regarding the laws of your state.

Law Encyclopedias

Each state in the U.S. has an encyclopedia outlining the laws and policies of the state which is called the "Jurisprudence" (example: "Florida Jurisprudence, Georgia Jurisprudence, etc.) You can usually find your state's law encyclopedia in your local public library. All you have to do is ask the reference librarian for help. If your local library doesn't have a law encyclopedia, the librarian can help you figure out how to get one from another library.

Internet

There are a plethora of places on the Internet where you can get information about state and federal laws. Sometimes what works best is to go to Google and then type in whatever you want to know about and your state, like this:

Then you just hit "search" and let the Internet point you in a good direction.

STEP 6

MASTER THE ART
OF NETWORKING

Don't be afraid to talk to people. You'd be surprised how
many people you'll met in the checkout line at the grocery store!
You should always want to let people know what you're doing. As
a young person, realizing the power of your voice can be a little
intimidating at first, especially when communicating with adults.
One thing you want to watch out for is *Adultism*. This constitutes
behaviors and attitudes based on the assumption that adults are
better than young people, and entitled to act upon young people

without their agreement. We all know that one adult who thinks they know everything! However, don't let that stop you from exercising your voice. You definitely shouldn't be afraid to talk to adults. Most times, adults are usually interested in learning and hearing from young activists.

TEEN ACTIVIST SPOTLIGHT

Maitri Khera, 16, says:
"Don't be afraid. Be proud of and confident in what you stand for and you can change the world."

Create your Elevator Pitch

Preparing an "elevator pitch" for networking conversations and internship opportunities can work wonders. They can go a little something like, "I'm AJ. I'm a student at XYZ and am interested in…"

Being able to quickly describe yourself and your strengths is not always easy to do, but it's definitely something that can be developed over time. When I am speaking to someone or a group of people, I usually say something along the lines of, "Hi, my name is Chanice. I'm 15 and I am a Youth Activist, Author, and Speaker."

Invest in Business Cards

Imagine the look on people's faces when they see that a Teenager hands them their own personal business card. It's priceless! Not only are business cards a quick and easy way to give someone your contact info, but it gives a great first impression. If anyone ever thinks about you and wants to get in touch, all they have to do is pull out the business card that you gave them.

Your business card should consist of the following information:

- Full Name
- Contact Information – A Professional Email Address, Your Phone Number, Your Title, and First Name & Last Name
- An appropriate email address would be: firstnamelastname@emailcompany.com or firstname@yourwebsite.com. If your email address is something like: *candylover432@emailcompany.com*, you might want to get rid of it.
- Your Website and Your Logo
- P.O. BOX Address (optional) - You don't want people knowing where you live!

Create a LinkedIn Profile

LinkedIn has a similar setup as the popular social media platforms, but it is solely for professional uses. Your profile consists of a professional photo, details of your educational experience, internships, part-time jobs, and volunteer work.

You may be wondering "How is LinkedIn going to help me as an Activist?" Well, I once had another teen whom I'd never met before, reach out to me on LinkedIn. She sent me a message explaining that she was looking for ways to improve her activism skills. Based on my profile, I guess she figured I was a good person to reach out to, so I sent her a message back and gave her some advice. We are still in contact today!

Join Networking Groups

I'm going to say three words that might scare you: Make a Facebook! Once upon a time, I was a teenager who believed that Facebook was for "old people". That is until I made one and realized how beneficial it is. On Facebook, there are thousands of groups that you can join that are geared towards a certain topic.

Example

I live in Florida and I love being involved in activism, so I'm a member of groups such as "South Florida Activism" and "Women's March Florida Chapter". Within groups, you can post things pertaining to the group topic, communicate, and most importantly network with others.

Stay In Contact With the People You Meet

If you come across someone who you feel would be a great person to have in your life and on your activism journey, reach out to them! I have developed so many relationships all because I decided to reach out to someone. Whether it be through a phone call, email, or text, don't shy away from the great things that can come from connection.

In March 2017, I attended a women's conference called "Black Women Rise". At this conference, I decided to go to a workshop about Black Women in Law. My goal is to become a Criminal Justice Attorney, so of course that's what I naturally gravitated towards. The leader of the workshop was a Judge from Washington State. After the workshop, I decided to introduce myself to the Judge and we promised to keep in touch with each other. Fast forward to several months later, the Judge from the conference presented me with a wonderful opportunity where I got to host a virtual workshop called, "What Can a Teenage Girl Do?" at her *Color Of Justice* program. It was a one day event in Tacoma, Washington that encouraged 80+ girls ages 11-18 to pursue a career in law or the judiciary.   If you've ever heard of the saying "closed mouths don't get fed", this same concept applies to activism. If you want or need something, then you have to take the initiative and stay in contact with the people you meet! You never know what kind of opportunities you will receive.

Reach Out To Local Media

Once you've started doing your fabulous work in activism, you'll want to tell the world about it. Contacting your local media is a great way of getting started.

First, you should figure out why you are reaching out to local media. Next, you'll have to decide which media outlet is the best place to tell your story. Some forms of media are better at covering some types of stories than others. It may be easier to gain the support of a media outlet that has youth reporters, covers youth events, or already works with your school. Don't limit yourself to just one media outlet; try contacting several of them. Your local media might include:

- Newspapers – school newspapers, dailies or weeklies; papers with a specific target audience
- Magazines – weekly, bi-monthly, monthly, features or news etc.
- Radio – school, local or national news programs, and talk shows
- Television – morning, noon and evening news, local or cable talk shows

- Online publications, blogs and media websites

After you've decided which media outlet to target, pitch your idea for a story or an event to a reporter by sending an email.

<u>Ways to Contact the News:</u>

To contact a News outlet, you must first find their contact information. Below are some different formats you may come across.

1) *News outlet provides an email to submit your news tip/story.* The email address will usually be tip@___news.com or news@____news.com. You can simply copy down the email address and send them your pitch.

2) *Hosted submission box.* This is usually under the 'contact' section of the news outlet's website. This format is also very straightforward as you just copy and paste your story into the box on the website and press send.

3) *List of reporter/editor emails.* For this format, you would look through the list and find the reporter/editor you think would cover your story. For example, if your story is about a new gadget, you should probably send the email to the tech reporter.

Content

Your pitch email should include the following:

- Reasons on why your story is relevant to the news outlet.

- The main points of your story (Don't make it too long. Just get straight to the point!)
- Important Links where the reporter can learn more information
- Your contact information

Sample Email Template

Hi <u>("reporter name" or "editor" for general email),</u>

In this section you want to briefly introduce yourself and then state the main point and why you are reaching out in 1 paragraph or less using a detailed explanation answering who, what, where, when, and why. The body of your letter should be anywhere from 1-2 paragraphs. You should include important links to where the reporter can learn more information. Lastly, you want to conclude this letter by stating: For additional inquiries, please contact <u>(Your Name)</u> at <u>(Your Email Address)</u> or <u>(Your Phone Number)</u>.

Sincerely,
[Name]
[Email]
[Phone]

TEEN ACIVIST SPOTLIGHT

Lauren Woodhouse, 16

Lauren serves as a Teen Advisor for the United Nation Foundation's Girl Up Campaign for the 2017-2018 year. As a result, she had the opportunity to appear on Portland, Oregon's KATU2's "Kids Doing Good Stuff" Segment to discuss her experience being a Teen Advisor. The great part was that all she did was send an email!

Lauren Woodhouse appears on KATU News on Wednesday, Sept. 27, 2017.

Lauren says, "I knew I was fully prepared with my talking points, but still I was very nervous. I had been on the news before in the 6th grade, but I was very nervous about it this time because it was live."

When I left Rockford to move to Portland, my gramma said something kind of deep. She said, "'Now that you're going to be living in a big city like Portland, you're going to have to do something really special to get on the local news." It was really touching to think that now since I'm coming up on my fourth year of living here in Portland, being a Girl Up Teen Advisor is what fulfilled those 'special' requirements."

Be professional. Be assertive.

As a young person, it is imperative that you demonstrate you know how to act in a professional manner, even at your age. As a well-spoken, eloquent teenager you will stand out for your maturity. Here are some *Do's and Don'ts* of networking that every teen should know:

Do ✓:

- Make eye contact
- Smile
- Give a handshake
- Introduce yourself (A simple "Hi, I'm _____!" will do)
- Give your business card
- Follow up

- Think Win-Win- How can I help this person in their life and will they be able to help me too?
- Be Patient- Good things come to those who wait
- Engage

Don't ✗:

- Show that you're shy and timid
- Dismiss someone as unimportant
- Hijack the conversation
- Sit when being introduced. Always stand.

<u>Look for Mentors</u>

Have you ever met someone and thought, '*Wow, they inspire me*'? or '*I aspire to be like them*'. Those are the types of people you should ask to be your mentor. With networking you're not just talking to people for the sake of it. You're talking to build relationships and gain connections. A mentor is someone who can guide you and give advice. All you have to do is ask, "Would you be willing to mentor me in_____?" and your answer awaits

TAKE A BREAK
SOMETIMES

Imagine it's Friday night and you've just come back from organizing your first event for your awareness campaign. Hundreds of people showed up, and the event was an overall success. Then, when you got home you started feeling worried and doubtful. You know that you're doing as much as you can, but you still feel like it's not enough. You feel overwhelmed, frustrated, and angry. You know that fighting for your cause is an important part of your life, but it seems as if there is always a new problem for you to solve. This is a representation of *activist burnout.* Although there will be many joyful moments along your activist journey, you must understand that it won't all be fun and games. Sometimes there will be moments where you get extremely frustrated and unmotivated, so when you do feel this way, you should know it's time to take a break.

Activist Burnout is defined, and subjectively experienced, as a state of physical, emotional and mental exhaustion caused by long term involvement in situations that are emotionally demanding. Oftentimes, dedicated activists spend so much time fighting for their cause that they forget about their own emotional, spiritual, and physical wellbeing. You're probably experiencing activist burnout if you feel:

- Anxiety
- Guilt
- Isolation
- Irritability
- Anger
- Sadness
- Pessimism
- Disappointment
- Numbness

- Fatigue/Insomnia
- Lack of Motivation
- Physical Pain/Sickness

If these same symptoms go on for months or even years, you should consult a therapist, counselor, or medical doctor.

I must admit that I have experienced activist burnout myself. Sometimes, I would be under the impression that I could do everything, when in reality I cannot. Now, when I find myself feeling exhausted to the point where I can't do anything but mentally shut down, that's when I know I need to take a break.

Understand that Adversity is inevitable

Along your journey you are bound to come across some type of roadblock or problem. If you don't, then just know that is pure luck. Things are not going to be perfect, but the most important thing to remind yourself of is your "why". You've got a mission to accomplish and you can't let a bump in the road stop you from succeeding.

TEEN ACTIVIST SPOTLIGHT

Munira Alimire, 17, says:

As a young, Black, Muslim girl living in America, things can be hard and adversity isn't new to Munira. Here's what she has to say about facing, overcoming, and staying positive in the midst of adversity:

"1) Make a community. You have to be able to laugh, cry, and cheer with people who understand where you're coming from. It makes life and activism easier.

2) Take breaks. You can't *always* fight or try to fix the world, because you're human and you need to recuperate.

3) Find Opportunities. If I can always expand, I'm inspired.

Establish a Support System

Surrounding yourself with people who love, support, and understand you is a great way to alleviate activist burnout. Whenever you're feeling down, it's important to have someone that you can talk to.

Practice Self Care

Self Care can come in many different forms based on the individual, but the most important thing is to never neglect your basic needs. Getting enough sleep, eating a healthy and balanced diet, taking showers/baths, and maintaining your personal hygiene, etc. is essential. Sometimes people get so caught up with their work that they forget to do those little things, which isn't good self-care practice.

Learn How to Say "No"

As an activist there's a good chance that you'll become obsessed with taking up opportunities and supporting causes, but sometimes you've just got to say a simple, "No."

Scenario

David is a 16-year-old Junior attending his schools' club fair. Although he already has a large workload and he's the Student Government President, David still believes he has enough time to join a club. While he's checking out his club options, the President of the "Students for Youth Activism" club approaches him and asks if he would like to be the Vice President due to his great experience with activism. David says, "Sure, I'd love to!" A couple of minutes later, a representative of the "Teens Preventing Breast Cancer Club" comes up to David and asks if he can help them coordinate the community breast cancer awareness walk. David thinks to himself *"I can't pass up this opportunity"*, so he says "I'd love to help!"

You may be thinking, "Where did David go wrong?"
Answer: David got so excited and overwhelmed that he didn't even realize he committed to more than he could actually handle. What David should have done is put his priorities first then respectfully declined the generous offers he received.
If you ever find yourself in a situation like David's, always remember what your top priorities are.

Implement Self Affirmations

Self affirmations are the recognition and assertion of the existence and value of one's individual self. When you find yourself moving into a not-so-good mental space, affirmations can not only improve your mental health, but it can also lead you to having a better mood and mindset. Below are a couple of self affirmation exercises you can practice. The smallest things can make the biggest differences in your life:

- Start your day by writing down 10 things you are grateful for.

- As soon as you get up in the morning say, "Thank You" as a way to express gratitude for life and waking up another day.

TEEN ACTIVIST SPOTLIGHT

Mary DiMartino, 15, says:

Stay strong. Don't let others tell you what you are doing is pointless or wrong. Stand up for yourself. The best piece of advice I can give is to put yourself first. It is really easy to get caught up in helping others and being selfless and generous. This becomes easy to translate into your personal lives. Stand your ground and make sure that your friends and your activities don't control your life. You are so strong and caring and loving. Put you first and take care of you. You can't help others if you don't first help yourself.

UNSUNG

HEROES

TEEN ACTIVIST SPOTLIGHTS
EXTENDED

Throughout the book, you may have noticed the *"Teen Activist Spotlights"* that were dispersed in the different steps. Each and every one of the teenagers that I highlighted in this book are phenomenal which is why I refer to them as "unsung heroes". You may not know them personally, but they are all doing phenomenal work in their communities and beyond.

There have been way too many times where the hard work of young activists have gone unnoticed, so I'm making sure that no longer happens. Each and every one of the teenagers in this chapter are exceptional. They aren't the average teenagers who you would think of, but that's okay. So, without further ado, I introduce you to the trailblazers and leaders of our future.

TEEN ACTIVIST SPOTLIGHT

Jonelle Christopher, 17

I am passionate about being a leader. I feel like leaders are needed in today's society because there are so many influences that could deter people from reaching their ultimate goal. There needs to be leaders in each generation to keep others on the right track and encourage them to reach for their wildest dreams.

Being A GOAL Digger

Goal Diggers Inc. is a nonprofit organization in the state of Georgia. The organization is aimed at empowering young girls to chase their dreams, polish their unique skills, and prepare for post-secondary education. I saw young women in my community that were not very active or taking advantage of the opportunities that were offered to them. I had a feeling that peer to peer help with this issue would be more influential.

Our mission is to be the bridge of guidance for these young girls by making tools accessible such as college tours, enrichment programs, workshops, and networking opportunities with professionals accessible. We want each Goal Digger to not only serve their community, but to know that their goals are attainable and they can be at the top of their fields.

The ultimate goal for our organization is to ensure that all of the "Goal Diggers" can not only receive aid in preparing for the profession that they would like to go into after college, but also make sure that these women take their skills learned in the group and apply it to the workforce and community.

We offer a resource hub of scholarships, leadership camp applications, and much more! We work in the community by volunteering at nursing homes, holding charity drives, and giving back to the less fortunate. I have always been a servant leader. I lead by example while also helping others without seeking recognition. My love for serving others motivated me to start my organization.

I am also a member of a nonprofit organization called, 21st Century Leaders. This organization takes business professionals from different fields and puts these influential people in the path of high school students in Georgia to network with one another. 21st

Century Leaders encourages students to take on leadership roles, enhance their business etiquette, and serve their community through leadership. 21CL encouraged me to become a young entrepreneur and use my innate social and networking skills to start my own nonprofit. I was amazed at how much I grew from being in this organization that I saw fit for something similar in my community of Valdosta, Georgia. 21CL's summer institutes was just one of my summer destinations. I always was active during the summer, keeping myself busy with leadership camps and other networking opportunities. Once my friends saw all of the fun that I was having over the summer, they were curious to how I became so involved.

Goal Digger's resource hub is the main focus of my organization. It gives members the opportunity to see applications for these various camps, scholarship, and volunteer opportunities that they may have never seen otherwise. I felt that this was important in my community because of the recent high rate of crime. With an alternative to being out doing something negative, girls that join Goal Diggers can be maturing into young leaders. Goal Diggers started as a community group with big dreams. I filed a business formation through the State of Georgia to incorporate the organization and it was approved in August of 2017. I believe that starting my nonprofit organization is one of my greatest accomplishments. Goal Diggers not only helped me to fulfill my purpose of being a servant leader in my community, but it also helped me to help others to fulfill their own dreams.

Many times I don't feel like people are supporting me as an entrepreneur or my organization as a whole, but I have to remind myself that I am not working *for* the support of others, but *to* support others.

I would like to attend a prestigious HBCU and pursue a degree in Literature. I would like to use my degree and go to Law

School. After Law School, I would like to practice criminal law and eventually run for public office.

I think it is very important to speak on issues that I believe need to be brought to the forefront to make sure that people's voices aren't silenced. I feel the need to advocate for people that don't have the platform that I have or the confidence to express their beliefs and opinions. If no one speaks up for what they believe there would be no change in how things are being done.

Connect with Jonelle

@jonellec18 (Twitter)

@jonellechristopher (Instagram)

Jonelle Christopher (Facebook)

Dayalis Zamora, 18

I'm passionate about human rights, because I believe that every human being should be able to live their lives happily. Unfortunately, not everyone in the world acquires the comfort to be happy, whether that be by not being able to obtain an education, not able to receive the same opportunities due to their gender, sexual orientation, race, religion, or social standing. It has taken thousands of years for civilization to get to the point where it is now, but it would be quite uneducated to say that the problems of the world are solved, especially when there are new problems appearing every day. Hopefully, however, there will come a day when there is no need for an international human rights lawyer, but until then, that is what I want to be. It is my ultimate goal.

It would be misleading of me to say that there was a crucial, pivotal moment in my life where my opinions and views drastically altered to the point where I am today, because in actuality, life is like a stream that develops into a river, and then a larger body of water. My opinions and passions have come and gone, and they have developed over time. My passion for human rights grew slowly over eighteen years of viewing the world through another lens, (not necessarily my own) and analyzing why events happen the way they do.

The most important challenge that I still perhaps have not overcome concerning my choice to follow my passion is the underlying fear of failure; of not finding a good job that lives up to my expectations or perhaps losing a case after months of hard work. I am beginning to learn, however, that I must not greet failure with bitterness, but rather, welcome it in order to learn from it. The other challenges will be overcome through the passage of time.

"I, TOO" is a community made by and for teenagers for the purpose of being able to talk about the pressing issues of our day through the point of view of teenagers. It is supposed to be a free space where teenagers are free to express themselves. Nowadays, there is a lot of discrimination against today's youth due to the lack of experience that comes with being a teenager. However, I feel that it is important to give a voice to those who are going to lead the country someday because if you simply keep them silent until the moment that they're supposed to speak, how are they going to thrive?

My advice to teenagers looking to become activists is to find an issue that interests you, and find an organization that is currently fighting to solve that issue. If there is no organization out there, or it is not as interactive, create your own movement. Age is but just a number -- what matters most in life is the passion and drive to accomplish an objective, and if the issue is incredibly important to you, there is no telling what a determined person can do.

My activist role model is Amal Clooney, because I am able to relate to her story so much. She immigrated to the United Kingdom at a very young age, and she tried her best to excel in school. When you are an immigrant, there is greater emphasis on school. Currently, she is an international human rights lawyer who has worked ceaselessly on quite difficult cases, representing the human beings who do not have anyone who will fight for them, except for her. Amal Clooney inspires me because she has given me the power to see someone with a very similar background to mine who has achieved an incredible amount of accomplishments, and someone who is well-recognized around the world for her work and her drive to fighting for those who cannot fight for themselves.

Some of my greatest accomplishments would have to be starting I, TOO and allowing teenagers to be able to voice their thoughts on certain issues, as well as joining Girl Up, a campaign sponsored by the United Nations Foundation that works towards giving girls a chance at an education. Over the summer of 2017, I travelled to Washington D.C. with other girls involved in the program, and we were able to advocate for a bill that would allow girls who are currently displaced in refugee camps go to school. The bill has passed in the House of Representatives, and hopefully, it will be passed in the Senate, where it will be given to the president to sign into law.

Connect With Dayalis

Instagram -- @dayaliszamora

Twitter -- @dayalistweets

Website: itoo.dudaone.com

TEEN ACTIVIST SPOTLIGHT

Leslie Arroyo, 16

I am passionate about making sure that every girl no matter her race, religion, sexuality, or socioeconomic status gets the education she rightfully deserves. I am also passionate about making a difference within the Latino community, as I myself am a Latina and believe it is important for us to fully embrace our culture and realize all the potential we have and not let ourselves be put down.

There certainly was a turning point that led me to identifying my passions, and that was when I realized that girls in developing countries were restrained from obtaining an education due to the simple fact of their gender. This was truly shocking, but eye opening, and led me to find a way how I (a sixteen year old girl from a relatively small town) can change this. I then began to look for organizations I could somehow get involved with that had common goals, and that was when I came across the United Nations Foundation's campaign Girl Up. I immediately knew I had to become a part of it.

One of my greatest accomplishments without a doubt is becoming a Girl Up Teen Advisor. As a low income Latina girl who lives in this relatively small town, I believed I had a zero percent chance of ever becoming a Teen Advisor. When I found out I had been chosen as one of the 21 girls I couldn't describe all the happiness I felt. It felt amazing knowing that I had gained a platform to continue speaking out about the issues I cared about and truly have the ability to better the lives of girls around the world. It was even greater of

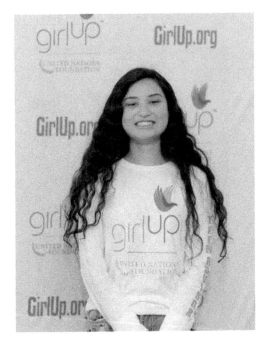

an accomplishment to start the first ever Girl Up club in my area, and have the ability to create change in my own community.

My goals for the future are to become even more involved with organizations or such that align with my beliefs and give me the chance of creating a difference. I also hope to get into a good college and later attend law school and become a lawyer. I especially dream of becoming a lawyer who deals with immigration cases and being able to start my own organization that sets out to help Latina girls and prepares them for success.

My advice for other teen activists is to be fearless to speak up about the issues you are truly passionate about. Do not let other people's views affect your own. Fight for what you believe in no matter what, and especially if you are like me from a relatively small town and a woman of color, do not believe you are not capable of changing the world because you certainly are. Go out and research every organization you would like to be a part of and do not shy yourself away from applying for positions or anything related. Also, do not be afraid of demanding change from your members of Congress. Instead sends them letters, call them, or set up a meeting with them and demand for change. No progress will be created if you do not speak up.

Connect With Leslie

Instagram: @leeslia

Twitter: @lesliearroyo21

Amanda Backal, 17

One issue that I am very passionate about is gender equality, specifically involving girls. Through my work with Girl Up, I feel as though I am able to help find and implement solutions to the problems that girls face internationally that affect both their wellbeing and the rest of the world. I believe that when a girl has access to education and is free from violence, poverty, and early marriage, she is not only more empowered, but is also able to make meaningful contributions to her community. She has the assets she needs to be an active member of society, thus helping to end the cycle of poverty. In this sense, I feel that girls truly are the future, because when given the resources they need, they have the power to do amazing things and shape the lives of others in a positive way.

Rather than having a specific moment which compelled me to take action on my ambitions and speak up about the things that I am passionate about, I attribute my drive to lead others and to have an impact on the world to many different people. I have been fortunate enough to have many friends and family members who, because of their ongoing support, enable me to make my aspirations a reality. My parents have raised me to believe in myself, to speak up when I have something important to say, and to always be open to learning new things. My sister, Ashley, and my friends have always inspired me; their intelligence, strength, and loyalty motivates me to be my best self. My teachers and mentors have offered me opportunities that open my eyes to ideas I'd never considered before and encourage me to work as hard as possible. These people have shaped my life and taught me the most valuable lessons that a single moment cannot capture.

Over the years, I have been fortunate enough to engage in many different opportunities in my community. I served on the Richmond Hill Youth Action Committee for two years, helping to plan events for youth in my community and guide the town on issues which affect youth. I have also served on the Richmond Hill Cultural Leadership Council for one year, which contributes to preserving and celebrating culture and diversity in my town, and on Student Council at my school for 3 years, this year as the co-president. Because of this work, I was awarded an Ontario Volunteer Service Award in May of 2017. I am also very proud of my work in the arts. I have acted in a variety of films, TV shows, and commercials and am a student of the Theatre Arts Mackenzie program at Alexander Mackenzie High School.

Of course, being a Girl Up Teen Advisor has been one of the greatest opportunities I have yet to engage in! I consider it a great accomplishment that I am able to work with Girl Up to fight for the rights of girls around the world and find concrete solutions to the problems they face.

When considering the future, I am definitely open to seeing where my current experiences take me. However, I do know that I want to do something that has a positive impact on the world. I believe that I am a powerful person and I can do anything I set my mind to (as everyone should). I know that no matter what I do in the future, I want to help other people and make the world a better place, whether that means providing aid to thousands of girls or simply inspiring a few people around me to take a stand against issues that matter to them. I know that the only way for me to feel fulfilled in the future is to be able to help others and make a significant difference in the lives of others, whatever that may end up being.

If I could give any advice to other teen activists, I would say to always remember the importance of education. The way I see it, education is the answer to almost every problem in some way. As an activist, you must acknowledge your responsibility to research the issues you're fighting for and to always look at issues and events from more than one perspective. Through thinking deeply about problems and questioning the ideals that you base your practices on, you are able to grow as a person and as a successful activist. Having a solid understanding of the views of other people can help you immensely in your journey to making societal change because you can develop an understanding of the roots of certain issues so you can develop targeted solutions. Learn as much as possible and always question the ideas you and the people around you believe. The more knowledge you have about all sides of your cause, the better.

TEEN ACTIVIST SPOTLIGHT

Alissa Flores, 18

I am passionate about giving girls the help I wish I got. For a period of time in my life, I struggled and I was afraid to speak up and ask for help. Even though the resources were there to get the support, I did not receive it the way I needed it. After overcoming my struggles I decided to take an initiative and provide help and guidance to girls.

In the past year, I have been blessed with the opportunity to help other girls, like me, through the humanitarian work I do with Girl Up. I try to picture and put myself in their shoes, I try to feel the emotions that run through them, the dreams, the wishes, and the struggles they have. I do this to find a form of help that is personalized to them. I think the best way to help others is by asking them what they need most and empathizing with what they have gone through. No one did that for me. I had to figure it all out on my own. If I would have had someone to help me the way I needed it, maybe I wouldn't have struggled for so long. However, I'm thankful for those struggles. I now know what I have to do to not only help myself, but other girls.

My life experiences led me to find my passions. As a first generation immigrant, I had to overcome many challenges that were thrown my way, including: the language barriers, the financial struggles, the color of my skin, and living in a new country that was now my home. However, these challenges gave me the tools I needed and shaped me to be the person I am today. For many years I have been wanting to help others, I just never felt I had the power to do so. Before I used to believe these were the obstacles holding me back. I'm just teenager, I have no money, and I'm still figuring who I am or how to survive in this crazy world. I was tired of wishing it and dreaming it, so I decided to do it. I realized the only thing holding me back were my doubts.

One day I decided to give activism a try, and when I did everything I always dreamed of fell into place. Now even as a teenager, with no money, and still in high school, I am helping girls in Malawi, Guatemala, Ethiopia, Liberia, Uganda, and India reach their dreams through the Girl Up Campaign by the United Nations Foundation. I use my voice and knowledge (the most important things you will ever have) to make a change in the world.

My most prized accomplishment is loving and being my true self, while embracing my Peruvian culture, my identity, my beautiful tan skin, and the diversity around me. I am no longer afraid to speak up, to use my voice, or to fight for what's right. I can now stand up for others and myself. I can march the streets of the Capitol to support what I am most passionate about, such as the Women's March, DACA, and LGBTQ+ rights. I'm not afraid to stand up for what I believe in.

Latinx Celebration at Hylton High School

I am also proud of the time when I organized the Latinx Heritage Celebration at my school. It was never done before, although my school has a Hispanic student population of about 31% and my county (Prince William County) has a 22% Latino population. I had to persevere and battle the obstacles presented to make this event come true. Thanks to the help of Mrs. Moulen, the wonderful librarian from my school, we humbly put together an event that celebrated the Latino heritage. I brought some decorations from home, placed it in a small part of the library, and placed seats around the area we had available for performances. When it was time for the event, a staggering amount of students from all over the school showed up. We had performances from dances, to poetry, to singing, to freestyling, and we even had the

149

audience come up and dance. The most rewarding part of this event was seeing the smiles, the joy, and the students feel so comfortable to come up and celebrate who they are.

Even though it was a small event everyone loved it. Students from ESOL expressed their joy and content to me, they felt accepted and embraced in a new country. That was the entire purpose of the event; to celebrate the students' culture and put a smile on their face.

Being a Teen Advisor for Girl Up

This year I was selected to be a Teen Advisor for the United Nations Foundation's Girl Up Campaign. It has been the opportunity that opened my horizons and truly pushed me to be myself, to celebrate the people around me, to be a globally minded citizen, and to change the world. Girl up to me represents who I am. It is what helped me accomplish my wildest dreams and to dream big. I would've never thought that I would change this world in such magnitude. I am given the opportunity to help Girl Up in these 5 core issue areas: education, freedom from violence, health, being counted, and leadership. I am changing girls' lives in Guatemala, India, Liberia, Malawi, Ethiopia, and Uganda. These girls are able to go to school safely, to have access to education, to help their communities, have access to health care, and most importantly have the opportunity to accomplish their dreams.

My goals and aspirations for the future are to continue making a positive change. During the Fall of 2018, I will be attending college and I hope to pursue majors in Communications and International Relations and minors in Spanish and Italian. I aspire to share the stories of others, to educate the public on important issues that impact us all, and to inform people why we must work together to solve them. I hope to bring cultural awareness through the art of film, in the future, as well. Whether it's about immigration, my Latino heritage, or girls' rights, film is a strong platform to educate the world around us.

The most important advice I would give to other teen activists is that nothing will ever be easy, but that doesn't mean you should give up. To be a good and successful activist you must learn about others' perspectives, put yourself in their shoes, and solve issues through human centered design. A good leader is one who critically thinks, who questions, and who takes every individual's point of view into consideration.

Connect with Alissa

Instagram @alissafloress

Twitter @alissafloval

TEEN ACTIVIST SPOTLIGHT

Fasica Mersha, 17

I am passionate about humanitarianism and activism, with a concentration on social issues such as race, gender, and sexuality. I think that one of the reasons that I am passionate about these things is because of how directly it affects my life.

My parents are originally from Ethiopia so I grew up hearing about the injustice in developing countries, which made me more observant of global issues. I have always been confronted by the issues of the world and the disadvantages I have to deal with because of it. I love the idea of fighting for what is right and being able to improve the lives of people like me worldwide. Being able to make the world a better place and helping people in need is the best feeling ever.

My turning point was the moment I decided to start my own Girl Up Club. Before I discovered Girl Up I was convinced that I wanted to be an engineer. I had always had an interest in social justice, but I didn't think I could have a career in it and I was more focused on making money than making a difference. When I started with Girl Up I truly realized how important social and political issues were and I felt a desire to be part of the change.

Girl Up showed me that it was possible for me to pursue meaningful work that can impact the world.

My biggest accomplishment would definitely be being accepted as a Girl Up Teen Advisor. The position as a Teen Advisor has provided me with endless opportunities that I would never have had access to, such as traveling to NYC and speaking at the UN or lobbying on Capitol Hill. I am also proud of the fact that I founded the Girl Up club at my school, and am the co-

founder of the Black Student Union at my school. I am currently the President of Girl Up and UNICEF, and Co-President of my Model UN and French Club, while also being the Vice President of the BSU.

Although my leadership positions are incredibly stressful I am very proud of how I have been able to grow as a leader and manage so many clubs that are very dear to my heart.

Right now, my main focus is trying to get into college. I don't know exactly what I will be doing in my future, but I do know that I want to be making change throughout the world. My goals include traveling and making as big as an impact on the world as I can.

The hardest thing about being a teen activist is the feeling that you'll never be able to accomplish anything. Teen activism is definitely one of the most daunting tasks, because it's hard not to feel like you can't do anything when the world is constantly treating you like you are incompetent. I think that the most important piece of advice that a teen activist should keep in mind is to ignore everyone else and take an initiative of the things that matter to you. Anything is possible if you put your mind to it, and don't underestimate yourself. I am a first generation black girl from a low-income home. I never thought I could become an activist until I discovered Girl Up. It's so easy to become discouraged by society that it often scares people from ever trying to be more than what people expect them to be.

I know everyone in my community was shocked to learn about all the things I accomplished. I was always the shy girl who wasn't the smartest in the room, so the idea of me being selected as a national Girl Up leader shocked a fair share of people. The truth is, I was probably more shocked than everyone else. It is always important to have confidence in yourself and to believe in the impossible.

Connect with Fasica

IG: fmersha

Twitter: fmersha425

LinkedIn & Facebook: Fasica Mersha

TEEN ACTIVIST SPOTLIGHT

Chris Suggs, 17

My community of Kinston, North Carolina has been one of the most challenged communities in North Carolina. Throughout history, we've been hit the hardest with some extreme hurdles - from being at the center of the Civil War, to harsh economic struggles during the Great Depression. In recent history, we've been stricken with three devastating natural disasters: Hurricanes Fran, Floyd and Matthew, which caused extreme flooding and property loss.

Growing up, living in the aftermath of many of these issues, it's made me long to know and experience how great Kinston truly can be. We're a resilient community. We're still standing strong, despite all that we've been through. However, it would be so great for us to be able to completely heal from these challenges and truly be a prosperous community.

I believe that my curiosity, passion and enthusiasm to see my community vibrant and bustling is the reason behind my passion and dedication to being involved. It's why I work so hard to improve my city, empower my peers, and be a positive representation of what can come to Kinston.

I have a strong passion for service, leadership and advocacy — especially when it comes to serving communities here in North Carolina. From starting my own nonprofit organization, to being the youngest appointee to the North Carolina Governor's Crime Commission, being a leader and representative in my state is something I'm deeply invested in.

This work can definitely be challenging at times! For someone who is a young person, and runs a nonprofit focused on young people, surprisingly, a lot of my challenges and oppositions have come from adults. I've found that the best way to handle these challenges and oppositions is to continue doing the work and providing stellar examples of youth leadership and civic engagement.

Kinston Teens

Young people just want, and need, to be supported, engaged and empowered. Through my organization, I'm amplifying the importance of that. We're capable of not just being 'the leaders of tomorrow,' but also of today! Kinston Teens is providing opportunities for that.

One of the first challenges I faced when I decided to follow my passion and start my first nonprofit was adults telling me not to do it. There were so many people telling me that I should wait until I was older, or that I should go another route – such as joining another organization or starting as a school club first.

I was receptive of their "advice," but something about it didn't feel right, so I didn't follow it. I was confident that this is what I was destined to do, and what God intended for me to do. I'm so grateful that I stayed true to my passion and my mission.

I don't believe there was any specific turning point in my life that led me to identifying my passion. Although I come from a pretty poor family and humble background, my parents and family members have always stressed the importance of service and giving back. I remember at really young ages attending charity events with my mom, cleaning up streets in our neighborhood with my dad, or attending city council meetings with my aunt. They knew how important it was to care for your community and be civically involved, and they wanted me to have that same mindset.

I like to think of the idea that being 'comfortable' is something for the old, and the wealthy. Currently, I'm neither one of those. In 2014, I began to get uncomfortable with some of the issues affecting young people in my community. From increased crime and violence, to poverty and a lack of jobs, to issues in our local school system. When you're uncomfortable, you want to do whatever you can to change your environment so that you can be comfortable. With all of these issues affecting young people, I felt like the best solutions from these problems would come from young people. I decided to start Kinston Teens so that young people could have a platform to voice their concerns, serve in leadership positions, and make tangible differences in their lives and our community.

Once I got the organization together, I held a press conference at our local library and invited our elected officials, community leaders, parents, educators, and most importantly – young people. I described in great detail, the importance of youth-leadership, how Kinston Teens could be effective, and the roles I wanted everyone to play in it.

A major focus of Kinston Teens is civic engagement; getting involved in local government, ensuring that the voices of young people are heard, and holding our local leaders accountable. We've done this through a variety of mediums. One of our signature events is our Teen Town Hall. The purpose of this event is to give young people an opportunity to meet, connect with, share concerns and develop ideas with our local and state government officials.

We also lead, organize and coordinate programs such as an Adopt-A-Street Program, Adopt a Vacant Lot Program, mentorship programs at local elementary schools, voter registration drives, leadership development trainings and more. Through our programs, workshops, projects and speaking events, we've impacted the lives of over 3,000 young people. We continue to make a difference in the lives of even more, young and old, in our community and beyond.

Because of the opportunities, I've had to travel the country and be in national media. I've been able to meet and connect with so many young people from across the nation and world that are making differences in their own communities and impacting society in their own great ways. I've joined many amazing networks of young leaders and have so many new friends that are really changing the world.

My greatest accomplishment has been the success of Kinston Teens. As an organization, we've grown tremendously since I started it in 2014, and it has definitely exceeded my expectations.

Black Youth Network

In the Spring of 2016, I co-founded the Black Youth Network, a national nonprofit organization with an aim of connecting and empowering young African American Leaders that are using their talents to change the world. I realized that there are many powerful and impassioned young Black leaders, but there was no central network or support system for us all. As young, intelligent leaders (who are also black), we face unique challenges that only *we* can truly understand. We also encompass a unique *power* and *ability* to make things happen. Just imagine if we could leverage that collective power to make even greater things happen... that's the goal for Black Youth Network.

The purpose of the Black Youth Network is to connect and empower exceptional young African-American leaders who are challenging the status quo, improving their communities, and making positive contributions to the African-American culture and beyond. Black Youth Network seeks to connect influential African American youth to share their stories, exchange resources, and build a national network of young change makers who are passionate about making a difference.

I would tell any young person who'd like to make a difference in their community to find their passion, and use it as their mission. It is rewarding and meaningful when you're doing great work for a cause that you really care about. Being an activist can and will be challenging, especially being a young activist. However, when you're passionate about what you're doing, it gives you the strength to push through and not worry at all.

There are lots of ways to combine your passion and interests with your activism. Be creative and make things happen!

Leadership

I believe that the true measure of a leader is their ability and willingness to influence, motivate, and empower the people around them. Far too often, leaders get into their role and position of power and become complacent. I place a strong emphasis on the leadership quality of empowerment. True leaders share their knowledge, skills, resources and responsibilities with those around them so that they become uplifted, motivated and encouraged to lead as well.

Since starting Kinston Teens, I've been able to empower and share leadership roles with so many young people in and outside of our organization. Our organization is completely youth-focused and youth-led, and young people are the ones coordinating, initiating, and executing the programs of our organization. I take great pride in knowing that Kinston Teens has made an impact that is much bigger than me, and will hopefully be around for much longer than me.

I'm currently a freshman student at the University of North Carolina at Chapel Hill double-majoring in Political Science and African & African-American Diaspora Studies. I plan to return to my hometown of Kinston after college, and continue to work with Kinston Teens. I recently successfully managed my mom's campaign for election as a city councilwoman here in Kinston. I see myself running for election in our local or state government as well—either as Mayor or State Representative. It is my long-term goal to eventually lead a career in public service as President of the United States!

We are more than how we are portrayed in the media. We are more than what the haters, naysayers, and pessimists say we are. We are smart, gifted, bold and black. It is ABSOLUTELY okay to be you. Find your passion, perfect your craft, and pursue your dream.

Connect with Chris

www.chrisjsuggs.com Facebook/Twitter/Instagram: @chrisjsuggs

www.blackyouthnetwork.org

Twitter/Facebook: /blackyouthnet

www.kinstonteens.org

Facebook/Twitter/Instagram: /kinstonteens

TEEN ACTIVIST SPOTLIGHT

Angie Jiang, 17

I am passionate about intersectional feminist issues because as a woman of color my demographics' voice is underrepresented in policy making and political discussions. Women, the LGBTQIA+ Community, and People of Color have been treated like second class citizens for far too long and I hope to spearhead the movement to prioritize equality and diversity.

My turning point was in the protest at my school for more teachers of color. It was on us to speak up and stand up for ourselves since Madison Metropolitan School District had failed to do so. Only 4.8% of teachers are people of color and with such a diverse district it was our duty to lobby and fight for representation, and support each other throughout the process. Ending the cycle of poverty was a goal. Representation is for all and omits no one. Although my school is generally very diverse, with minorities making up more than 1/3 of the school, we have barely any teachers of color teaching core classes. Seeing the passion within my classmates and the necessity of change spurred me into action.

I am proud to be a Girl Up Teen Advisor. I will be attending Columbia University in the Fall of 2018 studying political science and international relations. I was a semi-finalist at the national tournament of Congressional Debate. I am also the debate captain, forensics captain, swim-team captain, and am the president of two clubs. I hope to enter either domestic or international politics with the hopes of implementing policy that will correct societal wrongs and improve equality in the future.

I urge teen activists not to give up. It's easy to become jaded as adults and allowing other teens to put you down, but just because you can't vote doesn't mean you don't have a voice. Fight hard and feel hard. Express empathy and kindness to all those you meet, ESPECIALLY to the opposition.

Connect with Angie

@angiejianggg on Instagram and @angiejiang on twitter.

ABOUT THE AUTHOR

TEEN ACTIVIST, AUTHOR, SPEAKER, AND BLOGGER

Chanice Lee is a Teen Activist, Author, Speaker, and Blogger. She is the Creator and Editor-in-Chief of The Melanin Diary, the #1 online global platform for social justice, history, politics, and more, written entirely by Black Teens. As a passionate Activist and Leader, she is an involved member of several organizations on the local and international scale. Chanice was selected to serve as a 2017-2018 Teen Advisor for Girl Up, a campaign of the United Nations Foundation dedicated to achieving gender equality.

Chanice is also an esteemed speaker and has shared her words of wisdom and encouragement on several occasions. In August 2017, Chanice hosted a virtual workshop called, "What Can A Teenage Girl Do?" at the first ever Color Of Justice program, a one-day event in Tacoma, Washington that encouraged 80+ girls ages 11-18 to pursue a career in law. She was also the youngest speaker at the Florida March for Black Women in Miami, Florida on September 30, 2017 and at the Women's March "Power To The Polls" rally also held in Miami in January 2018.

She lives by her own personal motto: "Educate, Inspire, and Empower" and her favorite quote is "The revolution has always been in the hands of the young. The young always inherit the revolution" by Huey P. Newton.

IMPORTANT

Resources for Youth and Student Activists

Campaigns, Organizations, and Websites that are dedicated to youth and student activists.

<u>Advocates for Youth</u> – This organization champions efforts that help young people make informed and responsible decisions about their reproductive and sexual health. Advocates believes it can best serve the field by boldly advocating for a more positive and realistic approach to adolescent sexual health. Advocates focuses its work on young people ages 14-25 in the U.S. and around the globe.

Black Youth Project 100 – BYP 100 is an activist member-based organization of Black 18-35 year olds, dedicated to creating justice and freedom for all Black people. We do this through building a collective focused on transformative leadership development, non-violent direct action organizing, advocacy and education.

CampusActivism.org – This is an interactive website that has many tools for student (and non-student) activists including an events calendar, over 150 online resources (things like organizing guides and issue related materials), searchable databases of people, groups, schools, email lists, etc.

Youth Activism Project – This organization promotes and supports youth-led campaigns in America and around the world that seek impactful solutions to the world's most pressing problems. It produces multimedia resources that build organizing and leadership skills in order to train young people to be influential change agents. It also creates a pipeline for lifelong local and global civic leadership guided by mentorship and sustained involvement from previous participants.

Democracy Matters – Democracy Matters is a non-partisan campus-based national student organization, which works to get big private money out of politics and people back in. It offers paid internships to undergraduates. Democracy Matters mentors the next generation of leaders dedicated to strengthening our democracy. Students organize actions and projects connecting pro-democracy reforms to issues of environment, civil rights, education, health care, foreign policy, and more.

Young Democratic Socialists – This organization is the nation's largest socialist student and youth organization and among its activities is educating and mobilizing youth and students to confront the student debt crisis and to increase access to higher education.

United States Student Association – This organization tracks and lobbies federal legislation and policy, and organizes students from across the country to participate in the political process, through testifying in official Congressional hearings, letter-writing campaigns, and face-to-face lobby visits between students and their elected officials.

Young People For – This campaign is a strategic, long-term leadership initiative, that was launched by People for the American Way Foundation to invest in the next generation of leaders and build a long-term national network for young progressives.

Student Peace Action Network – This org is a grassroots peace and justice organization working on campuses to end physical, social and economic violence caused by U.S. militarism at home and abroad.

Student Environmental Action Network – This coalition is a student and youth run national network of progressive organizations and individuals whose aim is to uproot environmental injustices through action and education.

Sierra Student Coalition – This coalition is the largest student-led environmental group in the country. With over 250 affiliated groups, the SSC educates, lobbies, provides trainings for organizers, and organizes outings.

Project Mobilize – This entity is an all-partisan network dedicated to educating, empowering, and energizing young people to increase civic engagement and political participation.

Million Hoodies Movement for Justice is a national network of students, artists, activists, and organizers working to protect and empower young people of color from mass criminalization and gun violence.

Feminist Campus is the campus program of the Feminist Majority Foundation and focuses on reproductive rights, women's rights, affirmative action, and LGBT rights through organizing, networking and educational advocacy at colleges, universities and high schools nationwide.

Dream Defenders is an uprising of communities in struggle, shifting culture through transformational organizing. They use strategic non-violent direct-action, issue advocacy, civic engagement and an unlimited creativity to develop the next generation of radical leaders to realize and exercise independent collective power; building alternative systems and organizing to disrupt the structures that oppress our communities.

Generation Progress is a national organization that works with and for young people to promote progressive solutions to key political and social challenges.

Global Youth Connect – This organization's programs provide young leaders (ages 14-35) from a wide range of ethnic, national, economic and religious backgrounds with opportunities to learn more about human rights and enhance their ability to take action on pressing human rights issues.

Junior State of America – The mission of the Junior State of America and the Junior Statesmen Foundation (JSA) is to strengthen American democracy by educating and preparing high school students for life-long involvement and responsible leadership in a democratic society.

Taking It Global – This is an online community for youth related to global issues and creating positive change. This platform shares community details, tools, resources, media, regions, and issues.

Free The Children – Free the Children believes in a world where all young people are free to achieve their fullest potential as agents of change. Free The Children is an international charity and educational partner, with more than 1.7 million youth involved in its innovative education and development programs in 45 countries. It runs a range of campaigns throughout the year.

Amnesty International – Amnesty International National Youth & Student Program is one of the largest youth activist programs in Canada with more than 500 groups across the country.

DoSomething.org – DoSomething.org is America's largest nonprofit for young people and social change. They have 1,425,974 million members (and counting) who kick ass on causes they care about. DoSomething.org spearheads national campaigns so 13 to 25 year-olds can make an impact without ever needing money, an adult or a car.

Youth Activists -Youth Allies Network – The mission of the YA-YA Network (Youth Activists-Youth Allies) is to provide training and leadership experience to prepare young people to become the next generation of activists in the movement for social and economic justice.

United We Dream is the largest immigrant youth-led organization in the nation. The powerful nonpartisan network is made up of over 100,000 immigrant youth and allies and 55 affiliate organizations in 26 states. They organize and advocate for the dignity and fair treatment of immigrant youth and families, regardless of immigration status.

Youth for Change is a global network of youth activists working in partnership with organizations and governments to tackle gender-based violence and create positive change for girls, boys, young women and young men.

The Trevor Project is an American non-profit organization founded in 1998 focused on suicide prevention efforts among lesbian, gay, bisexual, transgender, and questioning youth.

BRAINSTORM

_____
_____
_____
_____
_____
_____
_____
_____
_____
_____
_____
_____
_____
_____
_____
_____
_____
_____
_____

STRATEGIZE

_____
_____
_____
_____
_____
_____
_____
_____
_____
_____
_____
_____
_____
_____
_____
_____
_____

EXECUTE